Lincoln: A Very Short Introduction

Very Short Introductions available now:

For more information visit our website
www.oup.co.uk/general/vsi/

Allen C. Guelzo

LINCOLN

A Very Short Introduction

OXFORD

UNIVERSITY PRESS

Oxford University Press, Inc., publishes works that further
Oxford University's objective of excellence
in research, scholarship, and education.

Oxford   New York
Auckland   Cape Town   Dar es Salaam   Hong Kong   Karachi
Kuala Lumpur   Madrid   Melbourne   Mexico City   Nairobi
New Delhi   Shanghai   Taipei   Toronto

With offices in
Argentina   Austria   Brazil   Chile   Czech Republic   France   Greece
Guatemala   Hungary   Italy   Japan   Poland   Portugal   Singapore
South Korea   Switzerland   Thailand   Turkey   Ukraine   Vietnam

Copyright © 2009 by Allen C. Guelzo

Published by Oxford University Press, Inc.
198 Madison Avenue, New York, NY 10016

www.oup.com

Oxford is a registered trademark of Oxford University Press

Library of Congress Cataloging-in-Publication Data
Guelzo, Allen C.
Lincoln: a very short introduction / Allen C. Guelzo.
p.   cm.—(Very short introductions)
Includes bibliographical references.
Summary: "Abraham Lincoln was a fatalist who promoted freedom;
he was a classical liberal who couched liberalism's greatest
deed—emancipation of the slaves—in the unliberal language
of divine providence; he was a religious doubter who became a
national icon bordering on religion; and he was a rights-oriented
liberal who appealed to natural law when confronting slavery"
—Provided by publisher.
ISBN 978-0-19-536780-5
1. Lincoln, Abraham, 1809–1865—Philosophy.   2. Lincoln, Abraham,
1809–1865—Political and social views.   3. Lincoln, Abraham,
1809–1865—Religion.   4. Presidents—United States—Biography.
I. Title.
E457.2.G874 2009
973.7092—dc22
[B]   2008041654

1 3 5 7 9 8 6 4 2

Printed in the United States of America
on acid-free paper

Contents

List of illustrations

Maps

Introduction

No man could have loved fame more than Abraham Lincoln. "Oh, how hard [it is] to die and not be able to leave the world any better for one's little life in it," Lincoln once complained, and one of the rewards he cherished for issuing his Emancipation Proclamation of January 1, 1863, was the expectation that "the name which is connected with this act will never be forgotten." And fame, certainly, is what Lincoln won, not only in America but around the world. He is one of the five Americans who, we can confidently say, are known the world over, alongside George Washington, Thomas Jefferson, Benjamin Franklin, and Martin Luther King.

But the elements that explain that fame have varied from place to place, and even from era to era. To Americans in the years after his death at the hands of an assassin in 1865, he was famous for exactly the reason he himself most expected to be remembered, as the Great Emancipator of America's four million slaves. But the laurel of Emancipator proved a heavy one for the next American generation to hold over Lincoln's head. The slaves whom Lincoln freed in 1863 were Negroes, and the continued sway of white racial supremacy in the minds of the vast white population of the United States eventually created an insufferable tension between public policies that quickly re-bound the freed slaves and their offspring to a legalized apartheid, and praise for the man who, by freeing them, had created that tension in the first place.

And so the Emancipator's laurel would be replaced by a succession of substitute laurels, almost a cafeteria of laurels, in which Americans could choose the one for Lincoln that that best suited the politics or the preferences of succeeding generations—Lincoln the Savior of the Union, Lincoln the Man of the People, Lincoln the Martyr, and so forth.

It has become possible, under this heap of disjointed laurels, to despair of ever locating the man himself, the man as he really was. Lincoln himself did not help matters. In an age of compulsive diary-keeping, he kept not even a scrap log of daily reflection. He did not live to write a memoir, as his lieutenants, Grant, Sherman, Sheridan, and McClellan did, and the two short autobiographical sketches he wrote in 1859 and 1860 for campaign purposes were pressed out of him by the importunities of newspaper editors. His infrequent references to his past were unrevealing and, at times, a little irritated, as though he were suspicious of the motives of those who wanted to unearth details of his dirt-farmer background. To one nosy inquirer, he merely remarked, "I have seen a good deal of the backside of this world," and that was as much as he cared to say. The eight volumes of his *Collected Works*, laboriously pieced together by Roy P. Basler and his staff and published in eight volumes in 1953 as one of the great documentary editing accomplishments in American scholarship, are filled mostly with day-to-day ephemera that give little sense of what shaped Lincoln's thinking and values. The tedium of unremarkable letters and odd jottings in the *Collected Works* are, of course, punctuated by his powerful speeches and his great state papers. But even those communicate little of what shaped Lincoln's ideas, since only on the rarest of occasions did he take time to identify the sources he was drawing upon.

Lincoln was, as his friend and admirer, David Davis, once said, "the most reticent—Secretive man I Ever Saw—or Expect to See." His law partner of fourteen years, William Henry Herndon, agreed: "the man was hard, very difficult to understand, even by his bosom

1. Lincoln at Alexander Gardner's new Washington studio, August, 1863.

friends and his close and intimate neighbors among whom he associated."

But there *was* a man of ideas behind this determined, private shield, and those ideas might be glimpsed. Henry Clay Whitney, who met Lincoln for the first time in 1854, thought that the first impression Lincoln usually made on people was that of "a rough intelligent farmer." But Lincoln's longtime friend and colleague, Leonard Swett, knew better. "Any man who took Lincoln for a simple minded man would very soon wake [up] with his back in a ditch." He took up the profession of law in 1837, without having graduated from a law school (or any school, for that matter), but purely on the strength of his mastery of a few elementary law textbooks and the mentoring of John Todd Stuart, an influential lawyer who had taken a liking to the twenty-eight-year-old Lincoln. Yet he rose to become a successful attorney, with a practice that handled more than 5,600 cases in the state and federal court system of Illinois and the United States, and Whitney was awed by how Lincoln could become as "terrible as an army with banners" in cross-examination. "He understood human nature thoroughly, and was very expert and incisive in his examination and cross-examination of witnesses," wrote Whitney, "If a witness told the truth without evasion Lincoln was respectful and patronizing to him, but he would score a perjured witness unmercifully. He took no notes, but remembered everything quite as well as those who did so."

Lincoln's intellectual curiosity frequently overspilled even the professional requirements of lawyering. John Todd Stuart told a campaign biographer in 1860 that Lincoln had a "mind of a metaphysical and philosophical order—His knowledge of the languages is limited but in other respects I consider a man of very general and varied knowledge." Unlike many of his legal peers, Lincoln "has made Geology and other sciences a special study" and "is always studying into the nature of things." A British lawyer, George Borrett, who interviewed Lincoln as president in 1864, was amazed when Lincoln "launched off into some shrewd remarks about the legal systems of the two countries, and then talked of the landed tenures of England," then rounded the conversation off with some commentary "upon English poetry, the President saying that when we disturbed him he was deep in [Alexander] Pope." John Hay, one of Lincoln's primary presidential staffers, was just as amazed to find himself in "a talk on philology" with Lincoln, "for which" the president "has a little indulged inclination." And even in the last few weeks of his life, the president who was better known for reading aloud from joke books reminded the San Francisco journalist Noah Brooks that he "also was a lover of many philosophical books," and then reeled off a list of the most influential books in American and British philosophy—Joseph Butler's classic *Analogy of Religion* on natural law, John Stuart Mill's *On Liberty*, and even the formidable eighteenth-century Calvinist, Jonathan Edwards, on free will and determinism.

But politics was Lincoln's "heaven," and "on political economy he was great." Lincoln, wrote Herndon, "liked political economy, the study of it." As well he might, since Herndon remembered Lincoln's most intensive book-reading resting on the most "important ones on political economy" in the nineteenth century: John Stuart Mill's *Principles of Political Economy* (1848), Henry Carey's *The Harmony of Interests, Agricultural, Manufacturing and Commercial* (1851) and *Principles of Political Economy* (1837), Sir Herbert Spencer's *Social Statics: or, the Conditions Essential to Human Happiness Specified* (1851), and Francis Wayland's *Elements of Political Economy* (1837). In particular, "Lincoln ate up, digested, and assimilated Wayland's little work." That string of authors and titles will not be too easily recognized today, but in Lincoln's time, they aligned perfectly along the intellectual and literary axis of English-speaking liberal democracy. And it is along that axis that, at last, we have a key to understanding Lincoln as he understood himself.

Liberalism has come to mean in our times an unpopular combination of sentimentality, hedonism, and a selective conviction that problems are the fault of social systems and that solutions are the province of government. But in the European and American worlds of the nineteenth century (and in continental European political philosophy today), liberalism was the political application of the Enlightenment. Its basic argument was that government is not a mystery handed down from the heavens to a certain anointed few (like kings or dukes or princes), or an unchangeable river of experience, which could not be altered or dammed, and people are not born, like medieval peasants, with a certain unchangeable *status* which they must bear all through life (*noble* or *common, saved* or *damned, slave* or *free*). People are born with *rights*—"certain inalienable rights," as Thomas Jefferson put it in the Declaration of Independence—which they must be free to exercise as a natural aspiration of their humanity. Liberalism was thus passionately devoted to freedom, and especially the freedom to *become* anything that your talents and the free exercise of your rights open up.

That passion for *becoming* increasingly took the political form of republics rather than monarchies, and middle-class capitalism rather than Tory landowning. The English liberals, Richard Cobden and John Bright, understood that their struggle against the citadel of the British landowning aristocracy, the Corn Laws, was really "a struggle for political influence and social equality between the landed aristocracy and the great industrialists." The German liberal, Johann Jacoby, described liberalism in 1832 in the same dualistic colors: "two opposing parties confronting one another: on the one side, the rulers and the aristocracy, with their inclinations toward caprice, and their commitment to old, irrational institutions; and on the other side, the people with their newly awakened feeling of power and their vital striving toward free development." And it was a struggle, not merely for economic advantage but for a better world than the hidebound societies of dukes and baronets. "A republican government," claimed the great pamphleteer Tom Paine, "by being formed on more natural principles . . . is infinitely wiser and safer . . . securing freedom and property to all men, and above all things, the free exercise of religion."

Free *exercise* of religion, but *not* a religious authority. Liberalism was not necessarily the enemy of religion, but it was no more interested in taking guidance from divine revelation than it was from classical philosophy. Cobden, who embodied both liberalism's hostility to aristocrats and its passion for measuring merit and talent by middle-class financial success, offered "scanty evidence of anything like an intense spirituality in his nature; he was neither oppressed nor elevated by the mysteries, the aspirations, the remorse, the hope, that constitutes religion." The reverence of the liberal for reason weakened the liberal's desire for submission to, and conformity with, the public manifestations of religion: belonging to a church, baptism, the ritual of worship, personal ethics. This, in turn, usually led to an indifference or even hostility to the public privileges Christianity still enjoyed in Europe, and to toleration for dissident forms of religion—not because the liberal had a fondness for religious underdogs, but because no religion seemed to the liberal to be worth quarrelling over.

Once turned loose onto the plains of freedom, liberals were confident there would be no limit on how far the reasonable and humane mind could push the progress of human knowledge and accomplishment. Because liberalism saw itself as the embodiment of reason, humanity, and freedom, it was confident that its own success was irresistible, and that overweening confidence that whatever represented progress also represented the triumph of liberty was the closest thing liberalism allowed itself to prophecy. Alexis de Tocqueville, the scion of the minor French nobility, had his moment of liberal epiphany in 1829, listening to the lectures of the liberal historian Francois Guizot at the Sorbonne and realizing that history was a record of the movement of progress, and that progress had equality as its goal. "It is my belief," added John Stuart Mill, "that the general tendency is, and will continue to be, saving occasional and temporary exceptions, one of improvement—a tendency towards a better and happier state."

Or would it? The French Revolution, which began as a liberal movement in 1789 and then collapsed into a popular tyranny and yielded to an imperial despotism under Napoleon Bonaparte, splattered the reputation of liberalism with contempt, as did the stillborn republics carved by revolution from Spain's ancient empire in South America. Joseph de Maistre, a French aristocrat who survived the Revolution and Bonaparte, snarled in his *Study on Sovereignty*: "One of the greatest errors of this age is to believe that the political constitution of nations is the work of man alone and that a constitution can be made as a watchmaker makes a watch." The natural political state of humanity, he claimed, was monarchy: "it can be said in general that all men are born for monarchy" and "even those nations destined to be republics have been constituted by kings." With the defeat of Bonaparte at Waterloo in 1815, the old European political power rolled back over the map of Europe, reinstalling kings, redrawing boundaries, and devising leagues and alliances that would move at once to shut down any renewed upsurges of liberal revolt.

Of all the hopeful liberal experiments, only one large-scale example survived, and that was the United States. And, by the 1850s, it was becoming increasingly plain that even the United States contained within itself the seeds of illiberal self-destruction in the form of an aggressive and arrogant "Slave Power," which sought to fasten the legalization of human slavery to the rapid westward expansion of the American republic. It was in that indecisive decade that Abraham Lincoln first strode—in his homely, flat-footed, artless, and artful manner—to the front of the American national stage, to defend the idea of liberal democracy from its own American despisers. The biographies of Abraham Lincoln easily outnumber those written about any other single individual in the English-speaking world. This will be a biography of his ideas.

8

Chapter 1
Equality

The ambition of the Lincolns

Abraham Lincoln's forebears arrived in the New World in the 1630s, in the first great wave of English migration across the north Atlantic. The Lincolns had been a family of middling gentry in Norfolk, a county whose flat fenlands were a hotbed of Puritan religious dissent from the Church of England. But in the 1630s, official repression of Puritanism became increasingly violent, and the Puritans' underground leadership finally turned to the desperate expedient of setting up a commercial corporation on the shores of the little-known Massachusetts Bay to serve as a cover for a mass Puritan exit from England. Among the Norfolk Puritans who signed up with the Massachusetts Bay Company were three of the Lincolns from the Norfolk town of Hingham. One of them, Samuel, an eighteen-year-old weaver's apprentice, settled himself in a new Hingham, south of the principal Massachusetts settlement of Boston.

It is not certain that Samuel Lincoln was actually emigrating in pursuit of pure religion. Samuel Lincoln's father, Edward, had been kicked down the social ladder in 1620 when his own father left him only a pittance of the Lincoln property in Norfolk, and Edward's sons were reduced to service as weaver's apprentices. When the Puritan exodus to Massachusetts began a decade later, it represented as much an opportunity to recoup the lost Lincoln fortunes as it did to escape the inquisitorial curiosity of the established Church of England. Land was cheap in Massachusetts, unencumbered by entails and quit-rents, and required only a strong back to clear it. By 1649, the weaver's apprentice from the old Hingham had acquired his own land-holding in the new Hingham, joined Hingham's reformed church, and married, thus securing at once advantages earthly and heavenly, which he could never have inherited in England.

There was something in Samuel Lincoln's restless search for independence and prosperity that seemed to have stamped itself onto the Lincoln family character. Samuel's fourth son, Mordecai, carved out a new Lincoln domain in neighboring Cohasset, which included three mills and an iron furnace, worth more than £3,000. Samuel Lincoln's grandsons, Mordecai and Abraham, moved yet again, and by the 1730s acquired hundreds of acres in northern New Jersey and eastern Pennsylvania. Yet another generation brought the descendants of Samuel Lincoln to the Shenandoah Valley of Virginia, where they contracted marriages into the first families of the valley and moved into the front rank of Shenandoah landowners. Finally in 1782, yet another Abraham Lincoln, deciding that his 260 acres of prime Shenandoah farmland was still inadequate to slake the Lincoln thirst, propelled himself over the Appalachians to stake out as many as 2,000 acres of virgin Kentucky forestland.

It was there, however, that the spectacular and acquisitive rise of the Lincolns came to a halt. Sometime in 1785 or 1786, while clearing ground near the settlement of Hughes Station, Abraham Lincoln was ambushed and killed by a party of marauding Shawnee Indians. The story of Abraham Lincoln's murder was handed down vividly to every Lincoln thereafter: how Abraham had been shot down by a Shawnee while "laying up" fence rails, how the Shawnee marauder had snatched up Abraham's eight-year-old son Thomas as a prize, how Thomas's fourteen-year-old brother Mordecai had picked up his father's rifle and, taking aim at "a Silver ornament or medal" on the Indian's chest, shot the Indian dead.

It was a heroic story. (In fact, more than just creating a story, it fostered a pathological hatred of Indians in Mordecai Lincoln, who in later years was rumored to have indulged more than a little revenge-killing, "for the Indians had killed his father and he was determined to have satisfaction.") But heroism aside, the death of Abraham Lincoln was the most serious setback for any of the Lincolns since the disinheritance of Edward Lincoln a century and a half before, and not only for the loss of the head of the household. Kentucky, in the 1780s, was still a province of the state of Virginia, and governed by Virginia's laws of inheritance. The bulk of the property left over after sales and taxes went to young Mordecai; nothing went to Thomas Lincoln or his two siblings. So instead of the Kentucky migration opening up a new chapter in the expanding story of the Lincoln family, young Thomas Lincoln found himself at age sixteen right back where his ancestor Samuel had been in 1637, an apprentice, this time as a cabinet maker.

And a cabinet maker he might easily have remained, for there was something in the ancestral passion of the Lincolns for self-improvement that never seemed to have fired in Thomas Lincoln. His neighbors remembered him as "lazy & worthless ... an excellent specimen of poor white trash" who could barely read and write, "a piddler" who was "always doing but doing nothing great." Years later, one of Lincoln's friends, Ward Hill Lamon, would characterize Thomas Lincoln as "apparently the most shiftless of men, an unskilled carpenter, a careless farmer, a wanderer over the face of the earth, but, wherever he went, taking with him his proverbial 'bad luck.'" It was not that Thomas Lincoln was entirely immune to his forebears' restless pursuit of greener, or at least more plentiful, pastures. As early as 1803 (and probably with help from his brother Mordecai), he purchased a small plot of land north of Elizabethtown, Kentucky. In 1806 he married Nancy Hanks, and in February of 1807, the Lincolns' first child, a daughter, Sarah, was born. Thomas evidently decided to let cabinet making be a sideline after her birth and moved the family to small farm on Nolin Creek, near Hodgenville, Kentucky, to take up farming where his father had left off fourteen years before. And it was there, on February 12, 1809, that a son was born. And perhaps with consciousness that he was trying to pick up the threads of a livelihood that the Indians had cut short with his own father's death, Thomas Lincoln named the boy for his grandfather, Abraham Lincoln.

But try as he might, Thomas Lincoln was spectacularly unsuccessful in reconnecting to the ambitions of his Lincoln ancestors. White settlement of Kentucky had been originally managed by a land speculation outfit, the Transylvania Company, which undertook a haphazard series of land surveys in order to begin selling prime acreage to land-hungry Virginians like the Lincolns. (In the four miles surrounding the new settlement of Harrodsburg, hasty surveying created parcels of land in every imaginable shape known to Euclidean geometry.) By the time Thomas's son was born, Kentucky land titles were riddled with enough cross-claims and defective titles to keep a stateful of lawyers in business. Among those defective titles was Thomas Lincoln's. The Hodgenville farm turned out to have a lien against it from an earlier owner, and Thomas lost the property; he bought a smaller farm on Knob Creek, in the same county, but in 1815 a neighboring landowner claimed to title to the Lincoln property, and Thomas found himself embroiled in another suit to protect his land.

He eventually won that suit, but the winning seemed scarcely worth it. The Knob Creek farm was difficult land to make a living from. Half a century later, Abraham Lincoln would remember that this farm lay in a "valley surrounded by high hills and deep gorges," and on one occasion, after planting corn and pumpkins, a "big rain in the hills" flooded the valley and "washed ground, corn, pumpkin seeds and all clear off the field." It did not help, either, that Kentucky farming was increasingly becoming dominated by large-scale plantations that used the labor of black slaves to raise crops. Against big-time competition like that, a small farmer like Thomas Lincoln stood little chance for carving out any lasting commercial success.

Thomas Lincoln's solution to his problems was the classic Lincoln gambit: move again, this time to Indiana, where the federal government, under the terms of the Northwest Ordinance of 1787, had not only laid out secure land surveys that guaranteed secure titles but also banned the import of slave labor. In 1816 Thomas Lincoln gathered up his small family again and migrated north, across the Ohio River, to the thick forests of southwestern Indiana, where he had filed claim to a 160-acre quarter-section of "Congress land," for which he made a down payment of sixteen dollars. But even this time-tried resolution for the Lincolns' troubles seemed not to work for Thomas Lincoln. A second son, named Thomas for his father, was born but died within three days. In October 1818, Nancy Hanks Lincoln developed the "milk sickness," from drinking the milk of cows that had grazed on the poison white-snakeroot plant, and died. Thomas remarried in December, 1819, and it was his one stroke of good fortune that his new wife, a widow named Sarah Bush Johnston. with three children of her own, turned into the perfect nurturer for the two motherless Lincoln children. "She was a woman of great energy, of remarkable good sense, very industrious," wrote her grandson-in-law, August Chapman, "She took an especial liking to young Abe. Her love for him was warmly returned & continued to the day of his death . . . . Few children loved their parents as he loved this Step Mother."

It was just as well that young Abraham found so much affection from Sarah Bush Lincoln, because he certainly got little of it from his father. Clever boys, as Lord Blake once said of Disraeli, frequently get short shrift from their fathers, and Thomas Lincoln did nothing to disturb that rule. "Thos. Lincoln never showed by his actions that he thought much of his son Abraham when a Boy," August Chapman recalled, "He treated him rather unkind than otherwise." Not that the boy was entirely innocent of provoking his father's anger. Abraham was "one of those forward Boys" who "when a Stranger would Call for Information to neighbour's house . . . allways would have the first word," and this embarrassed Thomas enough that "his father knocked him Down off the fence." Where Thomas was barely literate, young Abraham "Showed industry in attainment of Knowledge," and Thomas occasionally beat him "for neglecting his work by reading." Thomas Lincoln had at least been willing to send Abraham to school so that "I should be well educated." But as Abraham Lincoln remarked years later, Thomas Lincoln's idea of being "well-educated" was limited to having "me cipher to the rule of three." Father and son even split over religion. Thomas Lincoln belonged to the Separate Baptists, a small Baptist sect, which, like the Lincolns' Puritan ancestors, preached absolute predestination—that God controlled all events, down to the smallest human choice. Young Abraham, by contrast, would mimic sermons, but without believing them. His stepmother remembered that "Abe had no particular religion" and "didnt think of that question at that time, if he ever did."

It has been easy to exaggerate the contrast between Thomas and Abraham Lincoln, as if exalting Abraham required the denigration of Thomas. The elder Lincoln might not have been a swift thinker, but he was not stupid. One neighbor remembered that "Thomas Lincoln the father of Abraham could beat his son telling a story—cracking a joke." For all of his intellectual limitations, Thomas Lincoln "had a good sound judgement" and was "Exceedingly good humored." And if he appeared complacent, it was because the political ideology of the new American republic suggested that Thomas Lincoln had much to be complacent about.

Jefferson, Hamilton, and Lincoln

When Thomas Jefferson wrote, in his preface to the Declaration of Independence, that "all men are created equal," he was simultaneously throwing down a philosophical challenge *and* offering a description of what seemed to have miraculously become the American norm in the eighteenth century. In classical philosophy, the general reality that governed human society was inequality, simply because inequality seemed to be the order of the universe. The moon, the planets, and the fixed stars all existed in an orderly hierarchy, all embodying ever-increasing degrees of moral perfection. So, by extension, should human society.

As soon as the seventeenth-century scientific revolution collapsed the notion that the heavens were fixed in a ranked system, but instead moved according to natural and mathematically measurable forces, the notion that people were born into permanent orders of social rank and hereditary privilege began to totter also. "The question who is the better man has no place in the condition of mere Nature," argued the English philosopher Thomas Hobbes in 1662. Even if we grant that some men are stronger, faster, or wiser than others, still "Nature hath made men so equal in the faculties of body and mind" that "when all is reckoned together, the difference between man, and man, is not so considerable." With the American Revolution, the final doom of hierarchy seemed to have struck at last. "Mankind being originally equals in the order of creation," argued Thomas Paine in his incendiary pamphlet, *Common Sense*, "there is something exceedingly ridiculous in the composition of Monarchy." What the Americans would establish was a republic; and "to love a republic is to love democracy; to love democracy is to love equality."

But then the question became, what *kind* of equality? In the eyes of Thomas Jefferson, equality was what emerged from a landscape of moderate-sized, free-holding landowners. "Corruption or morals in the mass of cultivators," he wrote in his celebrated *Notes on the State of Virginia*, "is a phenomenon which no age nor nation has furnished an example." The model for this republican "cultivator" might have been Jefferson's fellow Virginian, John Taylor of Caroline, who impressed a colleague as "the ideal of a republican statesman ... plain and solid ... innately republican—modest, courteous, benevolent, hospitable," but who was fundamentally "a skilful, practical farmer, giving his time to his farm and his books, when not called by an emergency to the public service—and returning to his books and his farm when the emergency was over."

Nevertheless, there turned out to be more than one way to practice equality in America. Benjamin Franklin, who arrived in Philadelphia in 1723 as a penniless printer's apprentice, was able to make a fortune in the printing business by age forty-two, and then retire to buy a large house, entertain lavishly, become a colonel in the Philadelphia militia, and dabble in gentlemanly scientific and philosophical pursuits, based on nothing more than his canny eye for the main chance. Jefferson had no personal quarrel with Franklin, but Franklin's income flowed from urban rental properties and a series of print shops he franchised in seaports on the northeast American seaboard and the West Indies—not agriculture. These port cities were, in the Jeffersonian imagination, places where the noxious mold of corruption, influence-peddling, and suspicious forms of illusory wealth, like stocks and bonds and real estate speculation, grew thickly in the pavements, and where a tiny elite of moneyed interests held large numbers of propertyless wage-paid workers in economic bondage. Neither Jefferson nor his fellow Virginia republicans regarded real wealth as anything other than land; any system of banknotes, bonds, and mortgages fostered chicanery, insider-trading, and corruption. It was only in the healthy atmosphere of rural agriculture, where independent farmers supplied their own food, their own clothing, their own wood, that Americans could sit secure from the return of despotism and monarchy.

Unless, of course, those farmers were black slaves. It occurred neither to Jefferson nor John Taylor of Caroline that there was something remarkably inconsistent about expecting the rural landscape to exude equality when the work force was composed of the descendants of Africans kidnapped to the tune of over 11 million in the preceding 350 years and sold into hereditary slavery in the New World. For both Jefferson and Taylor, equality was a creed for white men, and Jefferson fantasized alternately about race wars, which would end in the massacre of all the blacks, and schemes for emancipating and then expelling them from America entirely. But Jefferson also feared the landless immigrants and poor workers of the seaport cities as well, and in his republic, propertyless whites as well as slaves would be excluded from the political process lest their ignorance and poverty allow the wealthy and unscrupulous to bribe or corrupt their votes.

No one embodied Jefferson's fears more corrosively than the New Yorker who became Jefferson's bête noire in the new republic, Alexander Hamilton. Born in the West Indies in 1757 and climbing by the same native talents as Franklin, Hamilton parlayed his attachment to George Washington's staff during the Revolution into a career in law, a society marriage, and in 1790 appointment as the secretary of the treasury when Washington was elected the first president of the United States. Hamilton knew from painful personal experience how hard it was, even in America, to crack the tight little universes of power created by overly mighty rural families. As an illegitimate son (and thus the permanent outsider), he had no place in anyone's network of "cultivators." Hamilton looked not to agriculture or landholding to promote equality, but to commerce. By commerce, he meant manufacturing; and to finance manufacturing, he wanted to create a national banking system and a hedge of protective tariffs to keep cheap manufacturing imports out. And with an anxious eye cast over his shoulder at the specter of a still world-powerful British empire, Hamilton was convinced that, until the American republic possessed a worthwhile manufacturing sector, and with the financial sector to support it, the American republic could never be safe in its practice of equality, Jeffersonian or otherwise.

If Hamilton was Jefferson's nightshade, Thomas Lincoln was exactly what Jefferson had in mind when he glorified the rural "husbandmen" as the model of equality. Neighbors of the Lincoln family remembered that Thomas Lincoln "was satisfied to live in the good *old* fashioned way; his shack kept out the rain; there was plenty of wood to burn." He "had but few wants and Supplied these ... Easily." In Indiana the Lincolns "raised a fine crop of Wheat, corn & vegetables" and kept themselves "well Stocked with Hogs, Horses & cattle." Even their "clothing was all made at home ... from cotton & Flax of there own raising," nor did they bother with shipping their produce to distant markets. Thomas Lincoln raised only enough crops "for his own use" and "did not send any produce to any other place" except to exchange for "his sugar and coffee and such like." Thomas Lincoln might have seemed like a falling-away from the ambitious grasp of his Lincoln ancestors, but in the Tory republicanism of Thomas Jefferson, he had already arrived at the plateau of equality and had no need for grasping further.

It did not occur to Thomas Lincoln that his son might choose a different path to equality. "I was raised to farm work," Abraham Lincoln remembered. "Though very young," Abraham "had an axe out into his hands at once; and from that till within his twentythird year, he was almost constantly handling that most useful instrument—less, of course, in plowing and harvesting seasons." What the boy preferred to have in his hands, though, was a book. The list of what he had available was not long—"Websters old Spelling Book, The life of Henry Clay, Robinson Crusoe, Weems Life of Washington, Esops fables, Bunyan's Pilgrim's progress," according to Lincoln's cousin, Dennis F. Hanks—but the young

Lincoln "was a Constant and I may Say Stubborn reader." This made no practical sense to Thomas Lincoln. "His father having Sometimes to slash him for neglecting his work by reading," Thomas Lincoln snarled that getting his son away from his books was like pulling "an old sow" away from the trough. And as an ominous shadow of the kind of labor Thomas Jefferson relied upon, Thomas Lincoln hired out his son to neighboring farmers, and kept for family use whatever was offered as barter for the boy's labor. "I was once a slave," Lincoln remarked years later, "we were all slaves one time or another," the only difference being that "white men could make themselves free and the Negroes could not."

Lincoln, commerce, and politics

In 1830 Thomas Lincoln decided to tear up fourteen years of roots in Indiana and move to Illinois—not to some great new estate but to a moderately-sized claim that could provide starter farms for his son, stepson, and nephew. But once Abraham Lincoln came of age in 1831, he showed no interest in taking up farming on anything his father could offer him. Once he had helped his father and stepmother erect a modest shelter near Decatur, Illinois, Lincoln struck out on his own, and not for the acquisition of land. Denton Offutt, an entrepreneur with big plans and a bigger mouth, hired Lincoln to help take a flatboat of goods down Illinois's Sangamon River, down the Illinois River, floating from there out onto the Mississippi and down to New Orleans. Lincoln was now about to enter in the new world of commerce, credit and markets.

New Orleans was Abraham Lincoln's first sight of a larger outside world, since the Mississippi was the great commercial highway on which all American commerce west of the Appalachians flowed. In the sprawling, filthy marketplaces, he would meet languages, races, steamboats, pirates, prostitutes, European imports, wrought-iron balconies—and slaves.

2. Earliest known image of Abraham Lincoln, c. 1848.

Lincoln knew well enough what slavery was: this was, after all, what Thomas Lincoln had fled Kentucky to avoid. Even in the free air of Indiana and Illinois, transit laws and other legal dodges allowed slave-owners to bring their slaves over the Ohio and work them as though no one had ever heard of the Northwest

Ordinance. But it was in New Orleans that Lincoln saw slavery in the mass—slavery that labored in the killing humidity and heat of the Louisiana cane fields, slavery that begat an exotic biracial class of mulattoes, slavery that turned every obsequious Sambo by day into a potential throat-slitter by night, slavery on the auction block, spread-legged and naked. "By God, boys, let's get away from this," he snarled, turning in disgust away from a street auction, "If ever I get a chance to hit that thing, I'll hit it hard."

The loquacious Denton Offutt had opened a store on the Sangamon River town of New Salem, and once the flatboat trip had proven Lincoln's reliability, Offutt offered him a job, clerking in the store. In 1831 such an offer looked like pure gold. Sitting beside central Illinois's main river and occupying a prime location for farmers tempted to turn their surplus crops into cash money or barter-goods, New Salem bid fair to begin the same meteoric rise to commercial dominance that sleepy villages like Rochester had begun once the Erie Canal was dug across upstate New York by its shrewd and opportunistic governor, DeWitt Clinton. And clerking suited Abraham Lincoln perfectly: it gave him the opportunity to apply his sharp mental energies to the challenge of accounting. Mentor Graham, a local schoolmaster, thought Lincoln knew better how to run a business than Offutt. "He was among the best clerks I ever saw," Graham remembered. "He was attentive to his business—was kind and considerate to his customers & friends and always treated them with great . . . kindness & honesty. He in fact superintended & managed Offuts whole business." But Lincoln also found time to indulge his favorite literary passions, starting with Shakespeare. Jack Kelso, another schoolmaster with whom Lincoln boarded, "was an Educated as well as a well read Man" and "deeply & thoroughly read in Burns & Shakespeare" and New Salemites remembered how Kelso and Lincoln "used to sit on the bank of the river and quote Shakespear" back and forth at each other. After hours in the store, Charles Maltby remembered Lincoln "occasionally reading the histories of the United States,

England, Rome and Greece" and his small collection of "the poetical works of Cowper, Gray and Burns."

But Lincoln used his wits for more public purposes, too. "The first time I saw him," recollected Mentor Graham, "was on Election day" and "we were deficient a clerk for the Polls," and Lincoln allowed himself to be drafted as clerk of elections. He soon became a favorite with the growing assortment of young, male get-aheads flocking into New Salem. One local roustabout, Jack Armstrong, heard Offutt boasting that he would bet good money that Lincoln could outwrestle anyone in New Salem, and Armstrong immediately rose to the bait. But once it became apparent that Armstrong could not gain the upper hand, the match was called, and Lincoln had earned his first measure of peer respect, "pitching quoits—jumping—hopping—Swimming—Shooting—telling Stories—anecdotes—and," Graham added, "not unfrequently as we in the west say—Setting up to the fine girls of Illinois." It was a solid mark of his popularity that when a disgruntled band of Sac and Fox Indians under Black Hawk tried to reoccupy lands in Illinois they had signed over to the smiling, threatening white politicians and soldiers, and New Salem contributed a company of militia to the campaign to round up Black Hawk's people, the militiamen unanimously elected Lincoln their captain.

In turn, Captain Lincoln impressed nearly everyone he met as a young man of curiously talented parts, on the way to success. "I fell in with Lincoln first when he was captain," recalled John Todd Stuart. "He was then noted mainly for his great strength, and skill in wrestling and athletic sports . . . a kind genial and companionable man, a great lover of jokes and teller of stories. Everybody liked him . . . he became very popular in the army." By the end of the Black Hawk incident, Lincoln had been convinced—if it took much convincing—to run, on the strength of the host of friends he had made in New Salem and in the militia, for the Illinois state legislature. He lost, but only because the

Black Hawk campaign had dragged on so far into the summer of 1832 that there was no time left for him to mount the hustings. And he was determined to take a second swipe at the polls at the next round of legislative elections in 1834. Mentor Graham remembered that "after the Canvass of 1832, Mr Lincoln turned his attention . . . to . . . History Biography & general newspaper reading." But Graham persuaded him that he would never be able to induce people to vote for him if he didn't understand enough of the rules of grammar to make impressive speeches, and so Lincoln "Commenced to study the English grammer with me," turning "his immediate & almost undivided attention to" Samuel Kirkham's *English Grammar*. "I have taught in my life four or six thousand people as School Master," Graham said later, "and no one ever surpassed him in rapidly quickly & well acquiring the rudiments & rules of English grammar."

By 1834 Lincoln was ready to offer himself again as a candidate, speaking from porches and wagon beds in "that shrill monotone Style of speaking, that enabled his audience, however large, to hear distinctly the lowest sound of his voice." This time, he took second place in his district (his own local precinct in New Salem giving him a whopping majority) in a field of thirteen, and since the district was entitled to send the four top vote-getters on the election ticket to the legislature, Abraham Lincoln had earned his first victory in politics. Equality had not been enough to satisfy him. It was opportunity he wanted, and as a member of the Illinois legislature, opportunity is what he would get.

Chapter 2
Advancement

The penetration of the market

Abraham Lincoln was only six years old when the War of 1812 ended, and the only recollection Lincoln had of it was his mother telling him "to be good" to a weary militiaman, straggling his way along the road past the Knob Creek farmstead— which he did by giving the soldier a fish he had caught. Other people's memories of the war were not so simple. James Madison, Thomas Jefferson's anointed successor as president, had taken the United States into a second war with Great Britain, cheered on by aggressive Jeffersonians in Congress who blamed the British for inciting Indian resistance to white settlement and who hoped to seize and annex Canada while the British were busy fighting Napoleon Bonaparte in Europe. A motley army of untrained American militia and Regular army troops, led by a Tennessee lawyer-turned-general named Andrew Jackson, overran the Indian-held lands in the Southwest and cleared the path for white settlement of Alabama and Mississippi. They then turned and administered a humiliating defeat to a British invasion force at New Orleans. But elsewhere, apart from Jackson's victories, the War of 1812 was very nearly a catastrophe for the United States. Despite a handful of celebrated naval combats on the high seas, American commerce was swept off the seas. American efforts to invade Canada disintegrated in defeat and looting, all of which triggered a grim retaliation when a British invasion force landed in the Chesapeake and then proceeded to march leisurely on Washington and burn the capital.

It was not only military mishaps that covered the republic with embarrassment. For more than a decade, the Jeffersonians had labored to undo the financial innovations of Alexander Hamilton. They allowed the charter for Hamilton's national bank (the First Bank of the United States) to lapse; they obstructed federal funding for internal road and canal systems, on the grounds that these "improvements" only benefited the commercial classes and beggared farmers through taxation; and they sneered at manufacturing and finance. And they were then aghast to discover that American armies without roads and canals had to chop their way through the forests just to get to the Canadian border, that the drain on the Treasury was so great that Madison's administration had to go cap-in-hand to private financiers to bail it out of near-bankruptcy, and that independent farmers had no capacity for producing the weapons, uniforms, supplies and ships needed to keep the British at bay. "It is said," wrote one observer, "that hundreds of our ill-fated soldiers perished for want of comfortable clothing in the early part of the war of 1812, when exposed to the inhospitable climate of Canada. The war found us destitute of the means of supplying ourselves, not merely with blankets for our soldiers, but a vast variety of other articles necessary for our ease and comfort."

Once the war was over, a sadder-but-wiser President Madison proposed a series of correctives to the Jeffersonian policies that had so nearly cost the republic its life. First, in 1816 Madison called for the revival of Hamilton's plan for a national bank. This Second Bank of the United States would provide capital for public investment, issue (through its bank notes) a dependable and trustworthy paper currency for the nation, and pay the U.S. government a bonus of $1.5 million dollars annually. Second, Madison proposed to use the proceeds from the bank and from an increased tariff on imported goods to provide for the construction of a national turnpike system, to be funded by the annual bank bonus and the $650,000 the bank would pay the government each year in stock dividends.

Nor was Madison the only Jeffersonian who had been shocked silly by the War of 1812, and he found support in Congress in another convert from pure Jeffersonianism, Henry Clay of Kentucky. The war, declared Clay, had "satisfied me that national independence was only to be maintained by . . . cherishing the interest of the people, and giving to the whole physical power of the country an interest in the preservation of the nation"—and that meant federal funding for "a chain of turnpikes, roads and canals from Passamaquoddy to New Orleans," and protective tariffs to "effectually protect our manufacturers." The addition of steam power to manufacturing and to shipping, and the introduction of the steam-powered railroad served only to further cut the costs and the distances involved in developing a new domestic economy. In 1800, a traveler leaving New York City would require a week to reach Richmond, a month to reach Nashville or Detroit, and six weeks to cross the Mississippi. But the railroads and the steamboats, taken together with the new projects for canals and turnpikes, abolished rural isolation and brought what had once been unthinkably distant markets (and their commodities) to the doorsteps of what had once been the remote agrarian communities.

Farm households began to abandon their traditional household manufacture of shoes, cloth, and other goods in order to buy cheaply priced textiles and manufactured goods. In western Massachusetts between 1815 and 1830, households stopped spinning wool yarn and flax for their own use and began wearing inexpensive store-bought clothing. And to pay for their increasing dependence on those goods, farmers were forced to tease larger and more productive harvests out of their soils, employ cost-saving machinery, and eventually turn to single-crop agriculture, producing exclusive harvests of corn or wheat for distant and invisible markets. These same farmers increasingly turned to growing broomcorn, a coarse wheat-grain used for manufacturing brooms but useless for any other household purposes, for sale to merchants in New York City. For the first time, Northampton, Massachusetts, merchants began *importing* grain from New York to grind and sell to local households through the new canal locks on the Connecticut River at Enfield in 1829 and through the newly-opened New Haven–Northampton canal in 1837. Even the merchants themselves changed: by 1845 most of the goods in the stores of Northampton storekeepers came from New York City suppliers, rather than from the surplus production of farms in the region.

Few among the old-line Jeffersonians were pleased with the tempting penetration of commodities into the world of the righteous and independent farmer. Jefferson complained in 1825 (a year before his death, deeply in debt) that the Americans of these newer days "now look to a single and splendid government of an aristocracy" to rule them, "founded on banking institutions, and money incorporations under the guise and cloak of their favored branches of manufacturing, commerce and navigation, riding and ruling over the plundered ploughman and beggared yeomanry." An upset of agrarian stability would, in turn, bring in its wake an upset of the racial hierarchy of white landowners and black slaves on which Jeffersonian agriculture depended. As it was, the great Southern agriculturalists survived on the labor of their slaves, while playing for the cooperation of small white farmers on the basis of white racial solidarity. Like the "Young England" Tories who fought to the bitter end for the Corn Laws, their notion of the ideal social order was both Romantic and feudal. In the Tory universe of Lord John Manners,

> The Greatest owed connection with the least,
> From rank to rank the generous feeling ran
> And linked society as man to man....

Oh would some noble choose again to raise
The feudal banner of forgotten days
And live, despising slander's harmless hate,
The potent ruler of his petty state.
Then would the different classes once again
Feel the kind pressure of the social chain.

Nothing, however, threatened the constitution of that order more than the instability of the market. As one writer bitterly commented in a New England agricultural newspaper in 1829, "The market is a canker that will, by degrees, eat you out, while you are eating upon it."

But to others, the penetration of the markets—through the cheapening of production, wage labor, steam-powered transportation, and inexpensive start-up costs—promised a social and moral revolution equal to that of 1776. Onto the ancient stage of masters and lords and tenants and servants walked a new class of entrepreneurs who could convert their mastery of the new machines into spires of wealth that made the land-locked aristocracies of Europe look as archaic and fragile as stained glass. In England, a former textile apprentice named Robert Owen borrowed £100 and built a small factory in Manchester; by 1809, only twenty years later, he had built up an impressive conglomerate of cotton textile mills and sold the entire business for £84,000 in cash. Richard Cobden escaped into the world of commerce as soon as he came of age, starting as a traveling commercial agent and then building a fortune in textiles (all the while feeding his voracious intellectual curiosity with mathematics, Latin, and political economy). The factory system made the small investments of small merchants balloon outward at colossal rates of growth: "It was not five per cent or ten per cent," a later English politician was to say, "but hundreds of per cent and thousands of per cent which made for the fortunes of Lancashire." And from that growth, Cobden arrived at precisely the same conviction as Lincoln, that "the prosperity and happiness of mankind depend chiefly upon the cultivation and maintenance of the conditions most favourable to the pursuits of industry and trade," for only in such an environment could "the same chance for all" be made available to all in the "struggle for existence." "The Saint of the Nineteenth century is the Good Merchant," declared the Unitarian theologian Theodore Parker, "he is wisdom for the foolish, strength for the weak."

He was also mobility for the static—not only mobility across distances, but mobility up the economic ladder. Just as the American Revolution had abolished the notion of political hierarchy, so the Industrial Revolution destroyed the notion of social and economic hierarchy, so that the one seemed like the natural complement to the other. Equality was more than simply a common standing of citizens before the law; it was a baseline of opportunity from which everyone was free to make of themselves what they wanted and what they could. "It is the spirit of a free country which animates and gives energy to its labor," claimed Massachusetts congressman Edward Everett in 1830, and "gives it motive and intensity, makes it inventive, sends it off in new directions, subdues to its command all the powers of nature, and enlists in its service an army of machines, that do all but think and talk." The old Jeffersonians looked darkly at mobility, because it threatened to disturb the stability and permanence upon which the independence of the yeoman rested (not to mention stability and permanence which slaveholding required to keep the slave in bondage). To Lincoln's generation, however, stability was merely another word for stagnation, for the repression of talent and imagination. "I believe that *Free Trade in Ability* has a much closer relation to national prosperity than even Free Trade in Commodities," wrote the Mancunian inventor and industrialist James Naysmith. Cobden lauded "the love of independence, the privilege of self-respect, the disdain of being patronized or petted, the desire to accumulate and the ambition to rise." Equality was not the end point, but the starting point, and from there, self-improvement should rule the day. "Advancement—improvement in condition," Lincoln would say in 1859, "is the order of things in a society of equals."

Lincoln in the Illinois Legislature

Advancement was what was uppermost in the twenty-five-year-old Abraham Lincoln's mind when he sat for the first time in the Illinois state legislature in November 1834. "Mr Lincoln in reference to Internal improvements & the best interest and advancement of this State, said that his highest ambition was to become the De Witt Clinton of Ill[inois]," remembered Lincoln's best friend, Joshua Speed, and everything the freshman state representative turned his hand to seemed pointed in precisely that direction. Without waiting to be tutored in his role by any of the nineteen senior members of the legislature, Lincoln was on his feet within two weeks of arriving at the state capital in Vandalia to propose authorization for a toll bridge across a creek in Sangamon County. This was followed by a bill to lay out a state-funded highway from the state line with Indiana westward to Peoria, on the Illinois River, and thence to the Mississippi. Ten days later, he was proposing the construction of another state road from the west bank of the Illinois River over prairie land so untrammeled that the road surveyors would have to mark its path "by suitable stakes well set in the earth, and in the timbered land by hacks, and blazes upon the trees." All told, during the two sessions of Lincoln's first term in the legislature, he introduced (or sponsored) eight separate road bills. And this was only the beginning.

Funding such an ambitious program of road construction demanded a choice between increased taxation, borrowing on eastern financial markets, or liquidating public assets. Illinois's most obvious public asset was government land, which, unhappily for Illinois, was not owned by the state, but by the federal government, as a holdover from fifty years before, when all of the

Northwest Territory had been federally owned. As late as 1840, Illinois had a population of less than half a million people and only seventeen incorporated towns, and as much as twenty million acres of Illinois land remained in federal hands. A good many Illinoisans believed vaguely that the public lands should "be held by the Government, and used perpetually as grazing fields for their stock." But it made little sense to Lincoln to wait for federal land offices to sell off this bonanza in land piece by piece. "I go for distributing the proceeds of the sales of the public lands to the several states, to enable our state, in common with others, to dig canals and construct rail roads, without borrowing money and paying interest on it," Lincoln announced as he ran—successfully—for reelection in 1836. And he offered as a general resolution in the legislature "That our Senators be instructed, and our Representatives requested to use their whole influence in the Congress, of the United States" to secure a 20 percent premium for the state on federal land sales in Illinois, which would in turn become the funding for the new "internal improvement" projects.

And not just roads, either. In December 1835, Lincoln asked that "a select committee of five be appointed to inquire into the expediency of incorporating a company to construct a canal upon the valley of the Sangamon river." Then, reaching to imitate DeWitt Clinton and the Erie Canal, Lincoln backed the building of a ninety-six-mile canal to link Lake Michigan with the Mississippi River (or at least the navigable part of the upper Illinois River that flows into the Mississippi). This Illinois & Michigan Canal had been part of Illinois governor Joseph Duncan's first message to the legislature in 1836. Lincoln not only supported the Canal proposal, but cast the deciding vote in the legislature that saved the bill from a "kill" motion, and he spent the next four years defending the canal against its critics. "The canal was then the great Northern measure," he recollected in 1854, "and it, from first to last, had our votes."

3. A lock on the Illinois and Michigan Canal near Chicago.

Still, the critics were not without strength, since the initial funding for the canal (from the sale of 236,000 acres of public land) was quickly used up by the costs of blasting through limestone with only picks, axes, and gunpowder. But rather than suspend work or attempt to borrow from East Coast banks, Lincoln's solution was for the state of Illinois to create its own state bank, which was chartered by the legislature in 1835. Lincoln rejoiced in the work of the bank: "I make the assertion boldly, and without fear of contradiction, that no man . . . has ever found any fault of the Bank. It has doubled the prices of the products of their farms, and filled their pockets with a sound circulating medium, and they are all well pleased with its operations." The bank, in turn, would become the funding base for other, more ambitious "internal improvements," and in 1836, at the beginning of his second term, Lincoln spearheaded a comprehensive public projects bill worth more than $10 million, as well as a move to relocate the state capitol from Vandalia to Springfield.

"Illinois surpasses every other spot of equal extent upon the face of the globe, in fertility of soil; and consequently that she is endowed by nature with the capacity of sustaining a greater amount of agricultural wealth and population than any other equal extent of territory in the world," Lincoln argued. "To such an amount of wealth and population, our internal improvement system...would be a burden of no sort of consequence. How important, then, is it that all our energies should be exerted to bring that wealth and population among us as speedily as possible."

The prospect of that "wealth and population" was enough to persuade central Illinois voters to reelect Lincoln again in 1838, and by this time, he had became "conspicuous in bringing forward and sustaining" the development of Illinois. Only now, he had a political party with which to identify himself—the Whigs.

Lincoln and the Whig ideology

It was not advancement, but ensnarement that old-line Jeffersonians saw in the mania for "internal improvements," and they were quick to find themselves vindicated in 1819, when a bank panic sent the overall American economy into a corkscrew of foreclosures, bankruptcies, debt suits, and fire-sale liquidations of assets. "The bursting of the banking tumor left behind the sores of public extravagances, foolish public contracts, excessive taxation, and great private debts....," howled the old Jeffersonian, John Taylor of Caroline. "What has caused these debts? Banking, borrowing, taxing, and protecting duties." The most violent disgruntlement was directed at the Second Bank of the United States. "All the flourishing cities of the West are mortgaged to this money power," raged Missouri senator Thomas Hart Benton, "They are all in the jaws of the monster!" Benton's fury, shared by the Jeffersonian faithful, found numerous other targets. Banks that suspended specie payments—payment in hard coin to depositors who wanted their money back—were closed down by state legislatures in Pennsylvania and Vermont; in Ohio, anti-bank riots exploded in Cincinnati; Kentucky abolished its state bank and created a national loan office to assist distressed debtors.

Out of the national distress appeared a new generation of Jeffersonians, whose champion was one of the few real military heroes of the War of 1812, Andrew Jackson of Tennessee. Jackson had made his fortune as a planter, lawyer, and land speculator, but without any love of banks, corporations, or paper money, or for governments that relied on them to confect wealth "of no intrinsic value" out of thin air and common gullibility. He told the president of the Second Bank that he had no particular animus toward the bank, because he loathed all banks equally. In 1822 William Duane, the editor of Philadelphia's *Aurora* and a fierce critic of banks, floated Jackson's name as a potential presidential candidate, and two years later, as James Monroe prepared to step down as president (and the last representative in the White House of the generation of 1776), Jackson began acquiring a wave of endorsements from those state legislatures hit hardest by the 1819 economic panic. The front-runners, Henry Clay and John Quincy Adams, represented the new edge of pro-banking, pro-improvement thinking within Jefferson's old party; they did not welcome in Jackson an interloper who looked determined to undo everything in a new American economy, which they had labored under Madison and Monroe to build up. The election of 1824 proved that Clay and Adams were much less convincing to the American public than the pain of the Panic of 1819, and only by a fluke of the Constitution's rules on elections—Clay, Adams, and Jackson ended their race for the presidency in a three-way split that forced the decision into the hands of Congress—was Adams finally elected. But Adams's presidency was handicapped by the rumor that Adams and Henry Clay had struck a "corrupt bargain" to throw Clay's support behind Adams in return for appointment as Adams's secretary of state. Jackson never doubted for a moment that he ought to have been the winner, and in 1828, when Adams and Jackson faced off again for the presidency, Jackson won a resounding victory.

It was a victory in which Jackson clearly saw himself as the tribune of the "the humble members of society"—oppressed farmers, the unemployed artisans, and the old Jeffersonian enemies of expansive government—thus taking the same ground that Benjamin Disraeli's Tories took against Cobden and Bright in Parliament, the "old faith" of "property acknowledging . . . that labour is his twin brother" and the "heroic tradition" of "the high spirit of a free aristocracy." In much the same way, Jackson turned his presidency into a veto-machine of every bill that looked to provide federal support for manufacturing ("It is principally as manufactures and commerce tend to increase the value of agricultural productions . . . that they deserve the fostering care of the government"—and not otherwise), internal improvements ("The great mass of legislation relating to our internal affairs was intended to be left where the Federal Convention found it—in the State governments"), roads and canals ("The construction of roads and canals" amounts to nothing but "a scramble for appropriations . . . whose good effects must of necessity be very limited"), the sale of public lands for financing internal improvements ("Congress possesses no constitutional power to appropriate any part of the moneys of the United States for objects of a local character within the States"), and banking (a "corrupting influence . . . upon the morals of the people.") Especially banking: when the Second Bank of the United States applied for an early rechartering in 1832, Jackson not only vetoed the rechartering, but systematically began de-funding the bank by refusing to permit any further deposits of federal funds there. When he promised that "Independent farmers are everywhere the basis of society and true friends of liberty," the arms were the arms of Jackson but the voice was the voice of Thomas Jefferson.

To Henry Clay, however, this was the voice of economic ruin and political despotism, and in 1834, Clay split from the old Jeffersonian coalition to form a new political party to which he gave a name hallowed in English-speaking political history as the enemy of military and political tyranny (as well as Tory landlords): *Whig*. "The Whigs of the present day," announced Clay in a speech on the floor of the Senate on April 14, 1834, "are opposing executive encroachment"—meaning Andrew Jackson—"and a most alarming extension of executive power and prerogative. They are ferreting out the abuses and corruptions of an administration, under a chief magistrate who is endeavouring to concentrate in his own person the whole powers of the government" and to protect the "one unextinguished light, steadily burning, in the cause of the people, of the constitution, and of civil liberty."

It took Abraham Lincoln little time to decide who best spoke for him. To the young Illinois solon, Henry Clay appeared as the "beau ideal of a statesman," and the kind of commercial system Clay had been advocating for the past fifteen years was only a larger, national version of the state-funded transportation and commercial projects Lincoln had been promoting in Illinois. "From the life of Washington and the teachings of the Fathers of the Republic he imbibed those immortal principles which fired his heart to an honorable emulation and a true patriotism," remembered Charles Maltby, who had first met Lincoln in New Salem. But "the life of the great commoner and statesman, Henry Clay, and his speeches in Congress," was Lincoln's polestar in politics, "and from the teachings of that eminent statesman he received his first political lessons." It was from Clay that Lincoln first "formed and cherished those resolves and principles which had for their object and aim the enfranchisement of the oppressed, the elevation of free labor and toil and the amelioration of the race," and another New Salemite recalled that "Henry Clay was his favorite of all the great men of the Nation," to the point where Lincoln "all but worshiped his name."

Lincoln publicly identified himself with the Whigs while running for reelection in 1836. By 1839 Lincoln had become a Whig party wheelhorse, drafting strategy statements and emerging in the legislature as the man whom Jesse DuBois, a fellow Whig legislator described as "the acknowledged leader of the Whigs in the House" and one of the "two principal men we relied on in the Legislature to make speeches for us." He was, remembered Springfield lawyer Stephen T. Logan, "as stiff as a man can be in his Whig doctrines." And as one further step away from the coarse Jeffersonian world in which he had been raised and from which he had fled, Lincoln turned in 1837 to a new profession, the profession most closely identified with the protection of American commercial interests. He became a lawyer.

Chapter 3
Law

Lincoln turns to the law

For someone as deeply committed to the new worlds of
commerce opening up across Illinois, Lincoln's own record as a
merchant was laughably unsuccessful. He clerked for Denton
Offut in New Salem for a year before Offut found storekeeping too
sluggish and closed out, leaving Lincoln dangling. Black Hawk
chose that opportune moment to stage his reverse migration back
into Illinois, and the call of the governor for the militia to turn
out saved Lincoln from unemployment. But with a sizable bounty
from his militia service in hand, Lincoln went back into
merchandising in New Salem as a partner with William F. Berry in
running one of the town's three general stores. Lincoln promptly
overextended himself, buying up on credit the inventory of one
of the other New Salem stores. But the real problem was Berry,
who (according to another New Salem merchant, William G.
Greene) "was very trifling and failed." By 1834 Lincoln and
Berry were deep in red ink. Berry died in January 1835, leaving
Lincoln with the full weight of the store's debts on his shoulders,
and creditors demanding the liquidation of the store.

Lincoln was already trying to shore up his financial position by
taking side jobs (including surveying and the running of New
Salem's tiny post office). But with Berry's death, the store was too

much for Lincoln to carry alone. Everything Lincoln owned, including his horse, saddle, and surveying instruments, was seized by the county sheriff and sold off. (A tenderhearted New Salemite, "Uncle Jimmy" Short bought the surveying instruments at the sheriff's sale and gave them back to Lincoln so he could at least have the means to earn some sort of living.) The county surveyor, also taking pity on Lincoln, hired him as a deputy surveyor, so that between the post office, surveys, and his modest salary as a state representative, Lincoln could keep paying his bills—and his debts.

There were, however, other ways of "advancement" in a liberal economy, something that Lincoln had learned through his short service in the militia, where he was thrown together with a dapper young lawyer from the new central Illinois entrepôt of Springfield, John Todd Stuart. Born in Kentucky, Stuart was one of a new wave of immigrant professionals from the upper South who were crowding into central Illinois in search of the same "advancement" as Lincoln. Between 1828 and 1834, Stuart had established an up-and-coming law practice in Springfield and won a seat in the state legislature, and when he met Lincoln for the first time during the Black Hawk insurgency, he was impressed by Lincoln's "candor and Honesty, as well as for ability in speech-making." Stuart suggested that Lincoln turn his natural speech-making talents to the practice of law. Although Lincoln's first instinct was to put his energies into a campaign for the legislature, Stuart's point was well taken. Lincoln needed something more than just the part-time work of a rural politician, and law offered him the opportunity to wed speaking with a reliable income. So, "after the election he borrowed books of Stuart, took them home with him, and went at it in good earnest," all the while mixing "in the surveying to pay board and clothing bills." What Stuart discovered was that Lincoln "has an inventive faculty—Is always studying into the nature of things." By the fall of 1836, Lincoln had mastered enough from his reading—mostly Sir William Blackstone's *Commentaries on the Laws of England*, some legal form books, a few textbooks on pleading and evidence, and the Illinois statute books—that he applied for examination before the lawyers who rather loosely constituted the Springfield bar, and was duly licensed. Two days later, he appeared for his first client, and in March 1837 he left New Salem and moved to Springfield to serve as junior partner to John Todd Stuart.

Lincoln's law practice

Until the American Revolution, law in America was the province of judges, not lawyers, and the judges were in most cases simply local gentry with a smattering of legal literacy, serving as magistrates and justices of the peace. Professional men-of-law who aspired to make a living from defending civil or criminal cases were vanishingly rare; in 1775 there were only forty-five practicing attorneys in the entire Massachusetts colony. Nor was there much for them to practice upon. Jury trials were infrequent. Criminal cases were usually devoted to meting out punishments for moral or religious offenses, and the punishments were appallingly savage; civil cases were usually limited to matters of debt and inheritance. And the guiding principles for both were contained in the "common" law, a vague mass of legal precedent and traditional procedure in English-speaking jurisprudence that judges and magistrates interpreted and applied by their own lights, without consultation with legislatures.

The American Revolution, in throwing off British rule, suggested to some American minds that throwing off British common law might be an appropriate next step, especially since so much of common law was based on theories of royal sovereignty and awarded vast discretionary powers to JPs and magistrates. If, in the new atmosphere of liberal democracy, sovereignty flowed instead from the people, then the place where law should be codified should be in the legislature, in the form of rational and consistent statutes.

Sloughing off the authority of common law proved a good deal more difficult than it seemed. America's revolutionary elites did not mind questioning the authority of the king, but they did not welcome the subversion of their own legal standing by the revolutionary committees that erupted onto the streets of Philadelphia and Boston. Even as devout a revolutionary lawyer as John Adams could step down from his chair as vice president to tell the U.S. Senate that he would never have taken up the revolutionary cause if he imagined that the revolution would put down the common law as well as the king. The gentry lawyers of the Constitutional Convention in 1789 and the urban lawyers of the 1790s thus struggled to hammer out an Americanized version of British common law, and with enough success that Supreme Court Justice Joseph Story (who did "not believe quite so much in the infallibility of the Common Law as my brethren") could announce that the common law "has become the guardian of our political and civil rights; it has protected our infant liberties, it has watched over our maturer growth, it has expanded with our wants, it has nurtured that spirit of independence which checked the first approaches of arbitrary power, it has enabled us to triumph in the midst of difficulties and dangers threatening our political existence; and, by the goodness of God, we are now enjoying, under its bold and manly principles, the blessings of a free, independent, and united government."

What differentiated the common law taught by Blackstone's *Commentaries* and the liberalized common law embraced by Joseph Story was the erasure of *sovereignty* (in which the substance of criminal or civil proceedings were assaults against the king's peace) and its replacement by *property*, which American lawyers would take as the new form of sovereignty. And, not surprisingly, Abraham Lincoln's legal career, as it unfolded over the next quarter-century, would be wrapped almost entirely around questions of property rights. In his first year as a lawyer, Lincoln was on record in ninety-one cases—two-thirds of them concerned routine debt collections. Over the course of the next five years, 80 percent of his cases involved debt litigation, and even as his practice matured through the 1850s, between 50 and 60 percent of his clients were parties to actions over debts.

Together with other kinds of property-defense litigation— both personal and commercial, from mortgage foreclosures to trespass—Lincoln's law practice would devote nearly two-thirds of its time to property actions. Out of 5,600 cases handled by Lincoln between 1837 and 1861, only 194 involved criminal law, and only 17 of those were high-profile murder cases. By contrast, land disputes connected with the Illinois railroads became one of the most frequent—and lucrative—segments of his practice. As railroad-building in Illinois replaced canal-digging as the premier example of "internal improvements" in the 1850s, Lincoln represented six different Illinois rail corporations, including the largest of the Illinois lines, the Illinois Central Railroad, in fifty-two cases. (Evenhandedly, he also represented plaintiffs in suits *against* seven other railroads; in the case of the Tonica & Petersburg Railroad, he sued it three times and defended it four times,) He was not, strictly speaking, a "corporation lawyer." Even at the end of his active career as a lawyer, Lincoln was still accepting five-dollar trespass cases. But, as Henry Clay Whitney admitted, "I never found him unwilling to appear in behalf of a great 'soulless corporation.'"

Eloquence was the magic potion of trial lawyers in frontier Illinois, "for the mass of the people judged men more or less by the power of *talk*." Which was just as well in Lincoln's case, since his physical appearance was not going to win him any ground with a judge or a jury. At six feet four inches, and with most of his height in his legs, watching Lincoln in motion was like watching two stilts at work. Like his Lincoln forebears, his face was long, angular, and homely, with large cheekbones and deep-set eyes under a shock of thick coarse black hair. "He had nothing in his appearance that was marked or Striking," said one fellow representative, and another lawyer added, after meeting Lincoln for the first time, that he "might have passed for an ordinary farmer, so far as appearances were concerned."

But once he began speaking, Lincoln had an almost instinctual feel for how to persuade an audience. Joshua Speed remembered hearing Lincoln speak at a political rally in 1836, and "it seemed to me then, as it seems to me now, that I never heard a more effective speaker. He carried the crowd with him and swayed them as he pleased." Sometimes, Lincoln's sharpest tool was humor, for "when enlivened in conversation or engaged in telling or hearing some mirth-inspiring Story, his countenance would brighten up the expression would light up . . . his eyes would Sparkle, all terminating in an unrestrained Laugh in which every one present willing or unwilling were compelled to take part."

But an even more effective weapon was Lincoln's transparency of manner. "He was an artful man and yet his art had all the appearance of simple-mindedness," recalled John Todd Stuart. "Sincerity" was Lincoln's long suit before a jury. At the same time, Lincoln's "sincerity" had no parts of the gullible to it. His sharp and retentive memory enabled him to carry long skeins of witness testimony in his head, and then wrap any inconsistencies around a perjurer's throat, and his patient but relentless unfolding of a case made him a formidable opponent in front of a jury. "His reasoning through logic, analogy, and comparison was unerring and deadly," wrote William Herndon, who would become Lincoln's own junior partner in 1844. "Woe be to the man who hugged to his bosom a secret error if Abraham Lincoln ever set out to uncover it. All the ingenuity of delusive reasoning, all the legerdemain of debate, could hide it in no nook or angle of space in which he would not detect and expose it."

His law practice did not necessarily make Lincoln a wealthy man, but it certainly did not make him a one-shingle peoples' attorney, either. For most of his legal career, Lincoln was a circuit lawyer, journeying two times a year around the circle of county courthouses which made up Illinois's Eighth Judicial Circuit. He traveled in company with the circuit judge and the other lawyers of the district, and shopped-up cases at each courthouse as the little cavalcade of lawyers processed around the circuit. Lincoln and Stuart generally charged fees that ranged from $2.50 to $50 for a case; when Lincoln and Stuart dissolved their partnership in 1841, Lincoln entered into another junior partnership with Stephen T. Logan, but the fee range remained much the same. After Lincoln set up his own practice independently (and took Herndon as his junior partner) in 1844, an increasing proportion of his cases came in the state Supreme Court and the federal courts, where he was able to command retainers of up to $100.

Lincoln was not shy about collecting, either. "We believe we are never accused of being very unreasonable in this particular," he reminded one client, "and we would always be easily satisfied, provided we could see the money.... We therefore, are growing

4. County Courthouse at Mt. Pulaski, Illinois, one of the courthouses on the 8th Judicial Circuit where Lincoln practiced law.

a little sensitive on that point." (On at least seventeen occasions, Lincoln actually sued to collect unpaid fees, including a $5,000 judgment that he won against the Illinois Central Railroad in 1856.) By the 1840s, Lincoln's practice was generating personal income that varied between $1,200 and $1,500 per annum (compared to the salary of the governor of Illinois at $1,200, and circuit judges' salaries of $750), and he had accumulated savings of $9,337.90, which he invested in notes and mortgages and which generated an additional average income of almost $200 a year. He corrected one colleague who had "supposed Lincoln poor," saying, "I am not so poor as you suppose."

Law and power

Lawyering was more than just a living for Lincoln. The revolutionaries who constructed the American republic in the 1770s believed that their republic was likely to survive only if it could find some form of political or social adhesive that would take the place of the venal cement, which held monarchies together—patronage, kinship, deference, and outright corruption. They expected to find this new republican adhesive in virtue, which meant a self-denying, disinterested dedication to the welfare of the entire republic. The image uppermost in their minds was the classical, self-denying Roman glorified by Thomas Babington Macauley in his *Lays of Ancient Rome* in 1842—Cicero at the rostrum, Cincinnatus at his plow, Horatius at the bridge:

> Then none was for a party;
> Then all were for the state;
> Then the great man helped the poor,
> And the poor man loved the great:
> Then lands were fairly portioned;
> Then spoils were fairly sold:
> The Romans were like brothers
> In the brave days of old.

Confidence in the victory of virtue required granting to human nature a degree of credit that would have been unthinkable before the Enlightenment, nor did it entirely banish republican fears that the blandishments of vice and power might prove all too alluring. But even if "there is a degree of depravity in mankind which requires a certain . . . circumspection and distrust," wrote James Madison, "so there are other qualities in human nature which justify a certain portion of esteem and confidence," and it was upon those qualities that a republic could be justifiably erected. Without virtue, "nothing less than the chains of despotism can restrain them from destroying and devouring one another."

But the American Revolution was not even over before the feebleness of virtue began to yield to the passions for material acquisitiveness and interest-group politics. The federal Constitution of 1787 deliberately looked past any appeals to virtuous self-denial and created a three-way division of governmental powers—an executive president, a bicameral legislature, and an independent judiciary—which pitted each division against the other in the confidence that no one branch of the federal government would allow the others too much power. Restraining power by division was a less elegant means to preserving the republic than cultivating classical republican virtue, and it certainly gave no pleasure to Thomas Jefferson or Andrew Jackson, who preferred to see Hamilton and Clay as pimps, highwaymen, and leeches rather than merely opponents. But it did set the pattern for American civil law to see itself as an extension of the restraint-of-power strategy, rather than the inculcator of virtue. And it was this concept that was uppermost in the mind of Abraham Lincoln when, in January 1838 (after he had been licensed for little over a year), he delivered as a lecture his first long reflection on the role of law in a liberal democracy.

The lecture was written for yet another great agency of American oratory, the town lyceum (in this case, the Young Men's Lyceum of Springfield, one of a nationwide network of 3,000 such speech-making societies begun by Josiah Holbrook in 1826), and Lincoln took as his topic exactly the question of how to guarantee "The Perpetuation of our Political Institutions." His answer to the temptations of power was not an appeal to Jeffersonian virtue, but to the countervailing authority of law. Any glance around the American scene would reveal "accounts of outrages committed by mobs," leading to disgust across the republic with "the operation of this mobocratic spirit" and finally a resort to a dictator who, like Napoleon, would promise order but deliver despotism. The only preventative was for "every lover of liberty" to "swear by the blood of the Revolution, never to violate in the least particular, the laws of the country; and never to tolerate their violation by others."

> Let reverence for the laws, be breathed by every American mother, to the lisping babe, that prattles on her lap—let it be taught in schools, in seminaries, and in colleges;—let it be written in Primmers, spelling books, and in Almanacs;—let it be preached from the pulpit, proclaimed in legislative halls, and enforced in courts of justice. And, in short, let it become the political religion of the nation; and let the old and the young, the rich and the poor, the grave and the gay, of all sexes and tongues, and colors and conditions, sacrifice unceasingly upon its altars.

Nor was mob rule the only example of the threat of power Lincoln could summon up. Virtue itself could be converted into a species of power whenever fanatics of various stripes concluded that some higher authority than the law accredited them as moral, rather than political, despots. "Those who would shiver into fragments the Union of these States; tear to tatters its now venerated constitution; and even burn the last copy of the Bible" in order to promote some vision of the New Jerusalem were, no matter what their good intentions, as much a species of "this mobocratic spirit" as the mobs themselves.

The image of a society ruled by law rather than by power came readily to Lincoln through the broad reading he had done in the principal political theorists of liberalism in the nineteenth century. The "function of Liberalism," wrote Sir Herbert Spencer, "was that of putting a limit to the powers of kings," and then, if necessary, using law to put "a limit to the powers of Parliaments." Admirable as virtue might be on its own terms, in a world where not everyone was virtuous, something further was needed to stay the shadow of tyranny, whether that tyranny came in the form of kings or (as in Mill's phrase) the popular tyranny of the majority. "Inasmuch as all men are not influenced in their conduct by moral and religious principles," added Francis Wayland, "the interests of man require that law should be invariably executed, and that its sovereignty should, under all circumstances, be inviolably maintained."

Lincoln in Congress, 1847–1849

Beside mobs, kings, and Parliaments, Lincoln may have had another source of lawless power in mind during his lyceum address: presidents. Once having vetoed the rechartering of the Bank of the United States, Andrew Jackson redirected the deposit of federal funds into politically friendly "pet" banks, which promptly went on a speculative investment spree. But no sooner had Jackson retired from the presidency in 1837 than the spree collapsed, and on a scale that made the Panic of 1819 look juvenile. Banks suspended payments, loans were called in, and in Illinois the entire internal improvements program that Lincoln and the Whigs had constructed now imploded. In May, the Illinois State Bank stopped payment in anything but its own paper banknotes (which quickly lost more than half their value), and after two years of struggle to keep the internal improvements projects solvent, the legislature finally killed the projects one by one "to provide for the settlement of debts and liabilities incurred on account of Internal Improvements in the State of Illinois." Lincoln fought a determined rear-guard action in defense of the projects, but it was no use. "The Internal Improvement System will be put down in a lump, without benefit of clergy," Lincoln complained bitterly. "Whether the [Illinois & Michigan] canal will go ahead or stop is verry doubtful."

Still, the financial panic and the failure of the internal improvements schemes put surprisingly little dent in Lincoln's political prospects. Across the nation, blame for the economic collapse was laid squarely at the doorstep of Jackson, and Jackson's hand-picked successor to the presidency, Martin Van Buren. In 1840 the Whigs capitalized on the national backlash against Democratic policy and captured the White House for the venerable William Henry Harrison. Lincoln won a fourth term in the Illinois legislature that year, campaigning across the state for Harrison as a sort of "traveling missionary" for the Whig party, and cementing his place in the Illinois Whig ascendancy in 1842 by marrying Mary Todd, the cousin of John Todd Stuart and daughter of a prominent Kentucky Whig family.

Mary was not the first of the Todds to make a life for themselves in Springfield rather than Kentucky. Mary's older sister Elizabeth had married Ninian Edwards, the son of Illinois's pioneer governor, and in succession Elizabeth brought three of her younger female siblings to Springfield, marrying off Frances to Dr. William Wallace in 1839 and Ann to a merchant, Clark M. Smith. Mary's decision to marry Abraham Lincoln was the problem case. Ninian Edwards had sat with Lincoln in the Illinois legislature, and as much as he admired Lincoln's shrewd political judgment, he could not help sniffing that, socially, Lincoln was "Mighty rough." Mary, on the other hand, was highly cultured "witty, dashing, pleasant, and a lady," and she impressed the Springfield Whig ascendancy that gathered around the Edwards's fine home on "Aristocracy Hill" as bright and lively, "a good talker, & capable of making herself quite attractive to young gentlemen." Lincoln might be welcome there as an ally, but not necessarily as a suitor. Elizabeth Edwards thought Lincoln "was a cold Man—had no affection—was not Social—was abstracted—thoughtful." He "Could not hold a lengthy Conversation with a lady—was not sufficiently Educated & intelligent in the female line to do so." But Mary "saw in Mr. Lincoln honesty, sincerity, integrity, manliness, and a great man in the future," and since even the Edwardses admitted that Lincoln "was a rising Man," they allowed an engagement to go forward. Lincoln, for his part, "wanted to marry" (he had paid serious court to two women in New Salem already, Ann Rutledge and Mary Owens). But in Springfield, he "doubted his ability & Capacity to please and support a wife," and in 1841, whatever understanding Mary and Abraham Lincoln had was abruptly terminated. A disappointed Elizabeth Edwards admitted that "I did not . . . think that Mr L. & Mary were Suitable to Each other & so Said to Mary." But a year later, the two were reunited, and on November 4, 1842, they were married in the parlor of the Edwards's home.

What actually brought these two radically dissimilar young people back together has always been something of a mystery. Lincoln himself broadly hinted that the match had been "Concocted & planned by the Edwards family" and that "Miss Todd . . . told L. that he was in honor bound to marry her." Whether this meant honor in the form of abiding by his original proposal, or honor is the sense of political ambition is not clear, and perhaps it was both. Certainly, Lincoln paid a severe price for his honor. Mary might be charming and well spoken, but she was also "terribly aristocratic and as haughty and as imperious as she was aristocratic," remembered William Herndon. She had been raised to rule over a house full of servants and slaves, not to actually have to run it herself, which is what she would have to do on Lincoln's income. Mary Lincoln "couldn't keep a hired girl because she was tyrannical" and ran them off, nor could she get along with her neighbors, who became witnesses to waves of screaming matches and conspicuous spending. "This woman was to me a terror," Herndon wrote years later, "imperious, proud, aristocratic, insolent, witty, and bitter." But in one respect, Mary and Abraham Lincoln were entirely agreed: both thirsted for

5. Mary Todd Lincoln, daguerreotype, c. 1848.

political prominence. Within a year of their marriage, he was already positioning himself for a run for the U.S. Congress, quietly circulating letters to potential backers to inform them that "if you should hear any one say that Lincoln don't want to go to Congress, I wish you as a personal friend of mine, would tell him you have reason to believe he is mistaken. The truth is, I would like to go very much."

Lincoln was not the only Illinois Whig who wanted a seat in Congress. But in Illinois, Whigs could count on winning only one of the state's seven congressional districts—Lincoln's own home Seventh District—and so a rotation was established among ambitious Whigs that delayed Lincoln's entry into the lists until 1847. By that time, the political climate in Washington had shifted dramatically. William Henry Harrison's presidency lasted for only one month, before he died of pneumonia. The vice president who took office in his stead, John Tyler, hoping to create his own political movement, promptly betrayed every expectation of the Whigs who had elected him as Harrison's running mate. The Whigs had looked forward to seeing Harrison inaugurate four years of internal economic development; instead, Tyler agitated for the aggressive expansion of American territorial borders, especially the annexation of the breakaway Mexican province of Texas.

The Whigs made a renewed bid for the presidency in 1844 by running their old champion, Henry Clay. But Clay lost the election by a wafer-thin deficit of 38,000 votes, and the presidency instead fell to an ardent Jacksonian, James Knox Polk. Expansion, rather than development, was as much Polk's project as it had been Jackson's and Tyler's, and he not only endorsed the Texas annexation in the face of Mexican protests but sent U.S. troops to enforce a Texas-Mexico borderline farther south into Mexico. This was hardly short of bullying, and when an armed confrontation between Mexican and American troops occurred in April 1846, Polk at once demanded that Congress "recognize the existence" of war.

Polk expected the Mexican War to be short and popular. It was neither. An American invasion force bogged down in northern Mexico; American troops who moved as occupiers into the northern Mexican provinces of Nueva Mexico and California soon found themselves coping with anti-American uprisings;

and a plot to insert the exiled Mexican dictator, Santa Anna, into Mexico in order to bring down the Mexican government backfired when Santa Anna instead quickly took command of the forces fighting the Americans. Not even the officers in command of the invasion could summon much enthusiasm for what was clearly a trumped-up war of aggression. "As to the right of this movement," wrote Col. Ethan Allen Hitchcock in his diary, "I have said from the first that the United States are the aggressors. We have outraged the Mexican government and people by an arrogance and presumption that deserve to be punished."

The political resentments of the Whigs boiled over into public condemnation of Polk and his war, stoked to an even whiter heat by Polk's heavy-handed use of Democratic majorities in Congress to reduce tariffs on American manufacturing and eliminate the deposit of federal funds in *any* banks whatsoever. In the off-year elections of 1846, the Whigs upset Democratic control of the House of Representatives, winning 115 seats to the Democrats' 108, and turning the House into a Whig shooting gallery at Polk's administration. And among the newly elected Whig congressman, riding on a fat election-day majority of 55 percent in the Illinois Seventh District, was Abraham Lincoln.

Lincoln was as eager to distinguish himself as a freshman representative as he had been a decade before as a freshman in the Illinois legislature, and although he had come with notes in hand to give speeches on "the true and the whole question of the protective policy," his debut speech in Congress in December 1847 was a full-throated attack on Polk and the war. The president had gone to war on the grounds that American troops had been attacked on American soil; but was it really American soil? Or were the Americans willfully trespassing on Mexican territory on Polk's orders? Lincoln wanted an inquiry into "whether the spot of soil on which the blood of our citizens was shed…was, or was not" Mexican territory, and always had been "until its inhabitants fled from the approach of the U.S. Army." Three weeks later, he was again on the attack against Polk. "When the war began," Lincoln said, he believed patriotically that even if people had doubts about the justice of the war, they "should, nevertheless, as good citizens and patriots, remain silent on that point, at least till the war should be ended." But Polk's lieutenants insisted on converting every vote, even for supplies, into a referendum "expressly endorsing the original justice of the war on the part of the President," and Lincoln had had enough. Polk's justification was "from beginning to end, the sheerest deception." The war "was a war of conquest brought into existence to catch votes," and thus secure Democratic political dominance "by fixing the public gaze upon the exceeding brightness of military glory—that attractive rainbow, that rises in showers of blood—that serpent's eye, that charms to destroy." Military glory held no such charms for Whigs (or, for that matter, for English liberals during the Crimean War just six years later). "By the way, Mr. Speaker, did you know I am a military hero?" Lincoln asked in the midst of a speech in July 1848. "Yes sir; in the days of the Black Hawk war, I fought, bled, and came away," but the bleeding was done after "a good many bloody struggles with the musquetoes."

The war gave Lincoln and the Whigs more than just a stick to beat Polk with; it also gave them their own military hero to run for the presidency in 1848 in Zachary Taylor, who had commanded the American troops in Texas and won a celebrated victory at Buena Vista. Polk obtained a peace treaty in February 1848, but it did nothing to stopper a groundswell of popular enthusiasm for Taylor. Battered by a frustrating war and an even more frustrating Congress, the exhausted Polk had no intention of seeking a second term, and within a few months of leaving office, he was dead, probably from cholera. Taylor was elected president by a margin of 140,000 votes over Democratic senator Lewis Cass, as dispirited Democrats gave up New York, Pennsylvania, Georgia and Louisiana; in Illinois, where Democrats had out-polled Whigs by 12 percent in 1844, Whigs narrowed the gap to 2.5 percent.

Taylor's triumph, however, paid Lincoln no dividends. He briefly convinced himself "that there are some who desire that I should be reelected," but his anti-Polk campaign had been read back home as an antipatriotic campaign. The Whig party leadership only reiterated its plan to rotate candidates for the Seventh District, and Lincoln had to give way. He campaigned vigorously for Taylor, but the only reward he was offered was the governorship of the Oregon Territory, which he declined. After fifteen years in politics, Lincoln enjoyed no one's endorsement, held no worthwhile political office, and had discovered that the drudgery of work in Congress was "exceedingly tasteless to me." It "would be quite as well for me to return to the law," Lincoln sadly concluded, and find "advancement" someplace else.

Chapter 4
Liberty

Lincoln and the problem of slavery

Lincoln returned to Springfield, politically empty-handed, at the
end of March 1849. "I was clean out of politics and contented to stay
so," he later told his fellow-lawyer Henry Clay Whitney. "My
children"—Robert, the oldest, followed by William Wallace
Lincoln, born in 1850 and Thomas Lincoln, born in 1853—"were
coming up, and were interesting to me," and he had lost none of his
ambition for success in lawyering. He dabbled in writing poetry,
most of it eminently unmemorable, and took as much pleasure as
ever in the poetry of others. "In the Matter of Poetry," remembered
Henry Clay Whitney, he "was likewise very fond of [Oliver
Wendell] Holmes [The] Last Leaf" and "he likewise took from my
library once a copy of Byron & read with much feeling several pages
commencing with 'There was a sound of revelry by night'" [Byron's
'The Eve of Waterloo']. But even as he claimed to be "losing interest
in politics," Lincoln did not stay entirely out of the political fever-
lands—he campaigned for the doomed Whig presidential
candidate, Winfield Scott, in 1852, and delivered a heartfelt tribute
to Henry Clay at the request of Illinois Whigs after Clay's death that
same year. He was, as he wrote in 1859, "always a whig in politics."
But he stood for no more elections and applied for no more
political offices; he had become an also-ran. That is, until 1854,
when he was jarred out of his professional slumbers by slavery.

Lincoln's reawakening in 1854 as an anti-slavery politician has seemed so sudden that more than a few people have wondered whether it was simply another chapter in his search for an issue upon which he could ride to political prominence. Certainly, he seemed to have shown no overly strenuous interest in the slavery issue in the previous forty-five years of his life. Although the Whigs had always been noticeably less enthusiastic about slavery than Jackson's Democrats, they still had a sizable number of slaveholders in their ranks—Henry Clay had been an owner of slaves, and so had the Whigs' most recent presidential victor, Zachary Taylor—and Lincoln never found their slaveholding an obstacle to supporting either of them. If anything, he chided anti-slavery Whigs who threw their votes away on the "Liberty Party" in 1844 for costing Henry Clay the presidential election, and chided them again in 1848 for grumbling too loudly against the nomination of Taylor. In 1847 Lincoln even represented a litigious Kentucky slave-owner, Robert Matson, in a suit to recover a slave family whom Matson brought into Illinois (under the state's generous transit laws) to work a farm he owned in Coles County.

Yet, Lincoln insisted years later that "I am naturally anti-slavery. If slavery is not wrong, nothing is wrong. I can not remember when I did not so think, and feel." He told his longtime Whig political ally, Joseph Gillespie, "that slavery was a great & crying injustice an enormous national crime and that we could not expect to escape punishment for it." And he said to Robert Browne, a young Illinois acquaintance, that "the slavery question often bothered me as far back as 1836–40. I was troubled and grieved over it." In 1837 he protested the Illinois legislature's handling of pro-slavery petitions by declaring that "the institution of slavery is founded on both injustice and bad policy." And in Congress, one of his last projects was a bill that eliminated slavery in the federal capital. He had seen slavery at its worst in New Orleans as a young flatboatman in 1831—"the horrid pictures are in my mind yet"—and he reminded Joshua Speed that "I see something like it every time I touch the Ohio, or any other slave-border."

There is, therefore, no reason to doubt the sincerity of Lincoln's revulsion at slavery or its power to reawaken his dormant political powers. But it was a revulsion with multiple roots. As he said to Gillespie, he hated slavery because it made working men ashamed of laboring with their hands, because manual labor was "slave work." Owning slaves "betokened not only the possession of wealth but indicated the gentleman of leisure who was above and scorned labour." Lincoln also saw slavery as a direct obstruction of the *Free Trade in Ability*, which liberalism adored. "Most governments have been based, practically, on the denial of equal rights of men," he said, while "ours began, by affirming those rights. We proposed to give all a chance; and we expected the weak to grow stronger, the ignorant, wiser; and all better, and happier together."

Slavery, however, was the "one retrograde institution in America," and it was "undermining the principles of progress" and of liberal democracy, as Americans struggled to explain why in a nation of liberty, four million innocent people could be held in forced labor. Americans were "descending from the high republican faith of our ancestors" and "proclaiming ourselves political hypocrites before the world, by thus fostering Human Slavery and proclaiming ourselves, at the same time, the sole friends of Human Freedom." Slavery violated the natural rights to life, liberty, and the pursuit of happiness that the Founders of the republic had clearly believed were hardwired into human nature by its Creator. "The ant, who has toiled and dragged a crumb to his nest, will furiously defend the fruit of his labor, against whatever robber assails him," Lincoln wrote, and in just the same way, "the most dumb and stupid slave that ever toiled for a master, does constantly know that he is wronged." How, then, could Americans claim any longer to believe in life or liberty when, through slavery, they assailed those natural rights in millions of their fellow human beings?

The one thing that does not seem to have animated Lincoln's opposition to slavery was race, despite the obvious fact that slavery

in America, like slavery in the British West Indies, was limited to—
and was justified precisely *because* it was limited to—black
people of African descent. Although Lincoln never seems to have
embraced the kind of full-blown white racism that Romantic
reactionaries were promoting across Europe in the nineteenth
century—he thought that "no sane man will attempt to deny that
the African upon his own soil has all the natural rights that [the
Declaration of Independence] vouchsafes to all mankind "—he still
indulged in a common racial condescension toward what he
called "Indians and Mexican greasers" and "mongrels." Even into
the 1860s, Lincoln assumed that north America was to be the
"home" of "free white people," and that free blacks would probably
remain politically inassimilable. The "physical difference between
the white and black races," he predicted, "will for ever forbid the
two races living together on terms of social and political equality."
But he never actually spelled out what that "physical difference"
was; and whatever obstacle such a "difference" posed admitting
blacks to full civil equality, it offered no justification whatever
for arbitrarily depriving them of their natural rights (and thus their
enslavement). The question of civil rights belonged to a different
category from that of natural rights, Lincoln insisted, and he
was alarmed whenever his advocacy of natural equality looked
like it might be used as a bogeyman to wrap "nigger equality"
around him.

This was as deeply as Lincoln allowed himself to explore the
complexities of racial anthropology, and he offered no explanation
of the future to be expected if and when the end of slavery
arrived and created a vast population of newly freed black people
who would never be permitted by the white majority to enjoy the
same civil rights enjoyed by every other free American. The
solution that came first to his mind (as it had to Clay and many
other Whigs) was to follow the gradual elimination of slavery in
America with the prompt elimination of the freed slaves by
"colonization" back to Africa. But Lincoln was too candid to
claim that colonization was either practical or right. "My first

impulse would be to free all the slaves, and send them to Liberia, to their own native land." But, he admitted, the colossal logistical mess of a colonization plan made the idea seem fantastic. On the other hand, to give up on colonization would fly straight in the face of the racial animosity of "the great mass of white people" toward blacks. He could not, with a straight face, claim that white racism "accords with justice and sound judgment." But in a democracy, a "universal feeling, whether well or ill-founded, can not be safely disregarded." And at that point, Lincoln simply closed his mind to any further speculation and contented himself with regretting the existence of slavery in America in the first place.

Not that pushing speculation beyond that point would have done much good. American slavery was the creation of state laws in the fifteen Southern states where slavery was legal; there was no federal slave code, and the closest that federal legislation came to the subject of slavery was the Fugitive Slave Law of 1793, which authorized the rendition of runaways across state lines, the abolition of slave imports (after 1808), and slavery in the federal capital (which was actually governed by the slave codes of the two slave states, Virginia and Maryland, which surrounded the federal district). In every other respect, the federal government had no authority under the Constitution to reach over the legal dividing line between state and federal jurisdictions to tamper with slavery. (Maintenance of this firewall was one factor that drove Democratic hostility to Whiggish schemes of "internal improvements," the reasoning being that a federal government powerful enough to meddle in harbor-dredging, canal-digging, and road-building might one day decide it was powerful enough to emancipate slaves; the fact that the federal capital was the one place where legalized slavery was under the immediate jurisdiction of Congress was what led Lincoln to make his proposal for emancipation there in 1849.) There was no point in agitating for the abolition of slavery so long as the Constitution forbade the federal government from doing the abolishing. If anything, there could be real harm in jeopardizing the rule of law by trying to break through that dividing line—which is why Lincoln had so little use for wild-eyed abolitionists who burned the Constitution (as William Lloyd Garrison did in 1854) as a symbol of their frustration.

What the federal government could do, however, was prevent the further extension of slavery into the West. Lincoln operated on the not-inaccurate assumption that slave-based agriculture—which meant, for all practical purposes, the growing of cotton to feed the Industrial Revolution's insatiable appetite for textile production—wore out soils, and forced the gradual sell-off of slaves from older, played-out slave states to newer ones in the Mississippi River Valley. Since Congress had direct oversight of the organization of the great lands stretching west of the Mississippi, all that had to be done to assure the gradual extinction of slavery was for Congress to ban slavery's extension into the West, and allow slave-based agriculture in the Southern states to decline in profitability to the point where slaveholders would cut their losses and free their slaves as a no-longer-supportable expense.

"I hold it to be a paramount duty of us in the free states, due to the Union of the states, and perhaps to liberty itself (paradox though it may seem) to let the slavery of the other states alone," Lincoln explained in 1845, "while, on the other hand, I hold it to be equally clear, that we should never knowingly lend ourselves directly or indirectly, to prevent that slavery from dying a natural death—to find new places for it to live in, when it can no longer exist in the old." He was confident that everyone "agreed that slavery was an evil." But under the Constitution, slavery's opponents "cannot affect it in States of this Union where we do not live." On the other hand, he countered, the "question of the extension of slavery to new territories of this country is a part of our responsibility and care, and is under our control." What the next step would have to be, once Southerners came to see reason and emancipated their slaves, was a consideration Lincoln was happy to put off for another day.

The condition of liberal democracy in Europe and America

The 1840s were an unhappy decade for the cause of liberalism almost everywhere. The single major exception was the success of Richard Cobden and John Bright, after a campaign of seven years, in creating an Anti-Corn Law League in the British industrial center of Manchester and riding it to a successful repeal of the Corn Laws. The "Manchester School" (as Disraeli disparagingly named it) believed that the Corn Laws—a system of protective tariffs for English agriculture—were the chief prop of the landed aristocracy. True, the Corn Laws shielded English agriculture from foreign competition, and wore the patina of benevolence toward English farmers. But Cobden and Bright perceived the Corn Laws as an anti-free market strategy, disguised as noblesse oblige. The high price of bread, propped up by the Corn Laws, constricted urban workers' appetite for manufactured goods, and sapped the political power of the middle class that industrial manufacturing had created. Cobden, Bright, and the Anti-Corn Law League drove the demand for repeal relentlessly forward, until by 1843 they had distributed 12.1 million *Free Trade* tracts and leaflets, converted the Tory prime minister Sir Robert Peel, and in 1846 sent the Corn Laws down to defeat in Parliament.

Elsewhere, however, liberalism fared considerably less well. Liberal political revolutions erupted in Austria, Germany, Italy, and France, temporarily bringing a liberal Republic to power in France (with Tocqueville as minister of foreign affairs) and pushing the old regimes elsewhere close to the brink. But the revolution in France in 1848 was soon subverted by its president, Louis Napoleon, the nephew of Napoleon Bonaparte, and in short order Louis Napoleon transformed himself into Napoleon III and France into the Second Empire. The revolts in Italy, Austria, and Germany were put down, and the kings and emperors restored.

And in America, James Knox Polk's imperial adventure in Mexico ended with the ruthless annexation of Mexico's northern provinces of Nueva Mexico and California. It was a settlement that the most influential Whig newspaper of the 1840s, the *National Intelligencer*, believed "everyone will be glad of, but no one will be proud of."

No one had more reason to regret the annexation than the opponents of slavery, since it was widely understood that Polk had plunged the United States into the Mexican imbroglio largely in hopes of seizing new territory where slavery could be legalized, in just the same way that his mentor, Andrew Jackson, had evicted the Cherokee Indians from their tribal lands in Georgia and Alabama in order to permit the expansion of slavery there in the 1830s. Far from consenting to be asphyxiated within its pre-Mexican War boundaries in the South, slave-based agriculture had experienced a tremendous revolution in profitability, and since Southerners had contributed a fairly substantial share to victory in the Mexican War, they now expected to be rewarded with access to the newly annexed western territories for slavery. After 1848, it was an expectation that was going to be vigorously asserted.

Actually, the first rumblings of unease at the prospect of slavery's expansion westward were felt as early as 1819, when the territory of Missouri applied to Congress for admission to the Union as a full-fledged state—and a *slave* state (that is, one where slaveholding was legalized by state statutes). The petition was met at once by the objections of an anti-slavery New York congressman, James Tallmadge: Missouri was the first state to be carved out of Thomas Jefferson's momentous Louisiana Purchase (the upper American West, bought from France in 1803), and it held symbolic value for those who worried that whatever decisions were made in Congress about Missouri would become precedents for the settlement of the entire West. Tallmadge's objections were met with threatenings and posturings by Southern congressmen, and in the end it took an entire year to hammer out a compromise that divided the Louisiana Purchase along the longitude of 36° 30', reserving everything above that line for organization as free territories and states, and everything below for slave territorial and state organization. Happily for Free Staters like Tallmadge, five-sixths of the old Purchase lands lay above the Compromise line, and were thus secured against any importation of slavery; only one other slave state (Arkansas) was ever formed out of the little left to slavery in the Purchase. It was with this Missouri Compromise in mind that Lincoln had rested safely in the assumption that genie of slavery had been solidly corked into its Southern bottle, where it would die out on its own.

But the Missouri Compromise's reservation of most of the West for freedom was threatened, first, by the rebellion of the Mexican district of Texas against Mexican rule in 1835, and its subsequent petition for admission to the Union as a slave state, and then, second, by the annexation of northern Mexico after the Mexican War, which Southern states insisted should be kept open for the expansion of slavery as their reward for wrenching the "Mexican Cession" from Mexican hands. Both challenges touched off an uproar in Congress; both uproars were resolved by compromises. The admission of Texas as a slave state was balanced by the admission of Iowa as a free state. And in 1850 the Mexican annexation was settled by a concession, which allowed the organization of new territories and states in the annexed provinces on the basis of "popular sovereignty"—and that meant letting the settlers actually resident in the annexed Mexican provinces decide for themselves whether they wanted to legalize slavery or not.

The adoption of the popular sovereignty formula was one of those political moments in which a formula that means nothing is adopted by everyone in an effort to avoid looking a problem straight in the eye. No one knew exactly what was meant by "letting the settlers decide" for or against slavery, since the popular sovereignty doctrine failed to answer a number of key procedural questions. (At one point in the territorial or statehood process should the people make their decision? Should it be done by a territorial or state convention, or by a direct referendum of the people? And wouldn't each side then strive to import as many last-minute pro-slavery or anti-slavery settlers as they could in order to sway the outcome? Should the vote be taken before or after writing a territorial or state constitution? If before, what would be done with any slaves brought into the territory before the vote?) What was more, popular sovereignty avoided entirely the question of whether extending slavery was compatible with the principles of a liberal democracy—whether, in other words, it was right or wrong to tolerate the expansion of slavery *anywhere*. But since, as Lincoln ruefully observed, "the Union, now, as in 1820, was thought to be in danger . . . devotion to the Union rightfully inclined men to yield somewhat, in points where nothing else could have so inclined them."

And to all appearances, popular sovereignty at first appeared to work. California was admitted to the Union with a free-state constitution; territorial government for New Mexico proceeded under a pro-slavery mandate. It worked well enough, in fact, that one of popular sovereignty's principal promoters, Illinois senator Stephen A. Douglas, proposed to take it one step farther. The Missouri Compromise's reservation of the old Purchase lands north of 36°30′ for free-state organization had successfully barred slavery from entering those lands for more than thirty years. But the Missouri Compromise gradually became the kiss of death to any territorial organization there at all, since any effort to organize a free territory or state in the Purchase would almost inevitably meet with a Southern veto. This impasse vexed Douglas, who, though a loyal Jacksonian Democrat, still dreamed of profitable railroad-building and settlement schemes stretching westward from Illinois, none of which would ever be realized as long as Southern vetoes blocked the territorial organization of the West. So, in 1854, Douglas seized on the petition of settlers from the Nebraska plains for organization as a territory as the moment for proposing that the old Missouri Compromise be repealed—and that the Purchase lands could be organized according to popular sovereignty.

It has never been clear (and probably was not entirely clear in Douglas's own ambitious mind) whether his proposal was intended simply to anesthetize Southern objections and break the logjam preventing free-state development of the high plains, or to swing Southern support behind a presidential bid in 1856 by allowing popular sovereignty to give Southerners some false hope that they could establish slavery in lands from where it had been heretofore barred. Douglas, for his own part, was a Northerner, from a free state; but he indirectly owned slaves (through a trust agreement from the estate of his father-in-law) and any ambitions he had for the presidency were dependent on Southern support. Douglas, for his part, disclaimed any partisanship for or against slavery. If, Douglas claimed, any territory "wants a slave-State constitution she has a right to it.... I do not care whether it is voted down or voted up." And in the spring of 1854, Douglas brought a territorial organization plan— the Kansas-Nebraska Act—to the floor of the Senate, complete with provisions for canceling the Missouri Compromise and settling the enormous swath of prairie lands that comprised the Kansas-Nebraska district on the basis of popular sovereignty, and skillfully managed it all the way to adoption as law.

Douglas was wholly unprepared for the blowback of political rage that swept through the North over the Kansas-Nebraska Act. Northerners who had been noddingly content to give allow the cactus-deserts of the Mexican Cession to be organized under popular sovereignty now awoke with an appalled start to see Douglas happily attaching the popular sovereignty rule to Kansas-Nebraska (which had real potential for development), tossing aside the Missouri Compromise like waste paper, and

leaving nothing standing in the way of slavery's wholesale
expansion into the old Louisiana Purchase but a settlers'
referendum.

The Kansas-Nebraska Act, 1854

It was the Kansas-Nebraska Act, Lincoln said in 1860, and its
"repeal of the Missouri compromise," which aroused him "as he
had never been before." Lincoln had always been confident that
the problem of slavery would solve itself, provided it was given
no new room into which it could expand and refresh itself. That
expectation was now in jeopardy. Even though, in technical terms,
the popular sovereignty provisions of the Kansas-Nebraska Act
did not actually mandate the opening of the old Purchase
territories to slavery, it did the next worse thing, which was to open
up the possibility, based on the decision of a territory's settlers,
that slavery *could* be legalized there. Coming after thirty years of
an ironclad guarantee that this would never happen, Kansas-
Nebraska and popular sovereignty looked like a betrayal, not
(as Douglas imagined it) just a new way to get the old Purchase
lands humming with law and commerce. So when, in the summer
and late fall of 1854 Stephen Douglas returned to his home state
to stump for the reelection of his fellow senator and political ally,
James Shields, he found lying in wait for him a politically
reenergized and rearmed Abraham Lincoln, ready to challenge
him in a series of speeches that would contain the stuff of
Lincoln's arguments against slavery for the next six years.

First of all, Lincoln insisted, if we consult the original intent of the
Founders of the republic, we discover that the original architects of
the American order had always intended to eliminate slavery. The
steps they took to ensure this were gradual and indirect, but
they always pointed in the direction of extinction. The Kansas-
Nebraska Act implied that the Founders' strategy of elimination
was no longer the policy of the republic; if anything, Lincoln
complained, Kansas-Nebraska betrayed the intentions of the

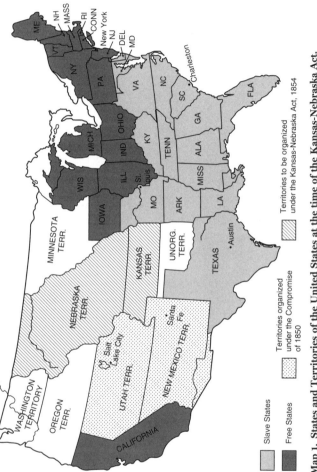

Map 1. States and Territories of the United States at the time of the Kansas-Nebraska Act.

Slave States

Free States

Territories organized under the Compromise of 1850

Territories to be organized under the Kansas-Nebraska Act, 1854

Founders by feigning indifference to slavery's spread, "practically legislating for slavery, recognising it, endorsing it, propagating it, extending it." This "is a woeful coming down from the early faith of the Republic," when "the policy of prohibiting slavery in new territory originated."

Slaveholders would respond, he knew, by claiming that no matter what the Founders may have thought in the 1780s, slaves were still their property, and not allowing them to take their property with them when they moved into the territories was a denial of their constitutional privileges and immunities. "This would be true," Lincoln conceded, warming to his second objection; but only "if negroes were property in the same sense that hogs and horses are. But is this case?" Obviously not. Slaves were human beings who had "mind, feeling, souls, family affections, hopes, joys, sorrows—something that made them more than hogs or horses." If blacks were only property, then why were there half-a-million free blacks living peacefully in the North? Would any other form of property be allowed to wander through the streets and highways of the North's cities without owners and tenders? Not unless, of course, they were not really property after all, but human beings.

And as such (Lincoln drove on) they possess natural rights—to life, liberty, and the pursuit of happiness, among others—that are outright contradictions of slavery. "Is not slavery universally granted to be, in the abstract, a gross outrage on the law of nature?" Lincoln demanded. "Is it not held to be the great wrong of the world?" How, then, could Douglas profess indifference to slavery being voted up or voted down if it contradicts both the Founders and natural law? What was worse, in a season when liberal democracy was everywhere on the run, what kind of message was the American democracy sending to kings and despots (not to mention the crowds of refugees who were fleeing them to America) when it renounced any ability to see a difference between slavery and freedom? Slavery "deprives our republican example of its just influence in the world—enables the enemies of free institutions, with plausibility, to taunt us as hypocrites—causes the real friends of freedom to doubt our sincerity, and especially because it forces so many really good men amongst ourselves into an open war with the very fundamental principles of civil liberty—criticising the Declaration of Independence, and insisting that there is no right principle of action but self-interest."

In the 1854 fall elections, Douglas's friends and supporters in Congress went to the wall. In Illinois, the state legislature was taken over by Whigs and anti-Douglas Democrats, and since U.S. senators were at that time still elected by state legislatures rather than by popular vote, Lincoln snatched at the possibility that a "fusion" of his old Whig colleagues and disenchanted anti-Douglas Democrats might pull together enough votes to dump James Shields and elect him to the Senate. But when the legislature met in February 1855, the Whigs could not deliver enough votes to Lincoln, and the anti-Douglas Democrats put up their own candidate, Lyman Trumbull. Lincoln withdrew, in order to allow Trumbull to be elected, on the grounds that this was better than allowing the reelection of Shields. But it was clear to Lincoln that his old party had failed him. In fact, it was failing across the country, as violent disagreements between Northern and Southern Whigs over the Kansas-Nebraska Act shattered party unity. By the spring of 1856, the Whigs were all but finished as a single, national party. And in June 1856, Lincoln was persuaded to transfer his allegiance to a new, all-Northern and unequivocally anti-slavery party, the Republicans.

Joining the Republicans was a riskier proposition than it seemed, since the Republicans were an unwieldy and possibly unstable coalition with only one issue to tie them together. The core of the coalition were old anti-slavery Whigs like Lincoln, still pleading for Henry Clay's "American System." But the Republicans also enlisted anti-Douglas Democrats who resented the arrogant hegemony of Southern slaveholders over the party of Jefferson and Jackson, as well as abolitionist radicals whom Lincoln had always viewed as no less a threat to the unity of the republic as Southern fire-eaters. They were united only in their fear of a dictatorial and aggressive "Slave Power" that had wrecked one national party, possessed the body of another, and now seemed content with nothing short of legalizing slavery all across the nation. Coming after the collapse of one liberal revolution after another, the "Slave Power" looked like nothing so much as an extension of the same resurgent aristocratic spirit that the Founders had once believed was on the run, the same reactionary rage that had bedeviled Cobden, Bright, and the Manchester Schoolers. More than just a plank in the South's politics, slavery was now assuming a far larger and more menacing shape, as a denial of the building-block principles of liberal democracy. Defenders of slavery in the 1850s moved beyond the conventional plea that slavery was an embarrassment, which had been wished on Americans by the British in colonial days, or an unprofitable burden, which white Southerners bore with economic Stoicism. Now, they crowed that slavery was a "positive good" for blacks and whites. Every civilized society, announced South Carolina senator James Henry Hammond, required a "mudsill" class, which performed the onerous tasks no gentleman would stoop to, and that Southerners had discovered that consigning blacks to this mudsill class as slaves meant freedom and liberty for whites. And anyway, concluded the Virginia slavery apologist George Fitzhugh, wage laborers in Northern factories were in a situation "infinitely worse than that of actual slavery." For Abraham Lincoln, however, these pro-slavery arguments were a categorical denial of the principles that had shaped Lincoln's entire life—of advancement, of equality, of the rule of law—and he yearned for the chance to strike a blow against the "Slave Power" that would knock it back into its Southern pen.

That chance was waiting for him in 1858.

Chapter 5
Debate

The failure of popular sovereignty

Contrary to the promises Stephen Douglas made for the popular sovereignty doctrine, almost nothing about popular sovereignty went right after the Kansas-Nebraska Act. Pro-slavery Southerners and anti-slavery "free-soil" Northerners were at once elbowing their way past each other to stake claims in Kansas and guarantee that any territorial referendum on slavery would be won by their side. Before "one Southerner gets ready to 'tote his traps, plunder, and niggers,'" boasted a Cleveland newspaper, "a dozen Northerners will be there ploughing before him"—to which Southern politicians responded by urging pro-slavery emigrants "to protect your own interests...with the *bayonet* and with *blood*." The first territorial elections, in November 1854, saw nearly two thousand pro-slavery Missourians cross into Kansas to stuff the ballot boxes and elect a pro-slavery territorial delegate to Congress. When voting for a territorial legislature began in the spring of 1855, more than 4,900 illegal votes (in a territory with only 8,500 settlers) were cast, electing a pro-slavery legislature, which at once began passing a territorial slave code. Free-Soilers responded to this fraud by electing an anti-slavery convention of their own, and sending their own anti-slavery delegate to Congress. This soon came to bloodshed by the end of 1855, culminating in a pro-slavery raid on the Free-Soil stronghold of Lawrence on

May 20, 1856, and the butchering of five pro-slavery settlers along Pottawatomie Creek three days later by a New England–born abolitionist named John Brown. Far from guaranteeing a peaceful settlement to Kansas, popular sovereignty had only invited a bloody struggle for dominance.

Yet worse tidings for popular sovereignty were on the way. In March 1857, the U.S. Supreme Court handed down a decision in the appeal of a Missouri slave, Dred Scott, in a freedom suit that had been winding its way through the court system for almost a decade. The slave of an army doctor, Scott had been transported onto federal property, and into residence at Fort Snelling, in free-soil Minnesota; Scott believed that the moment he had been taken onto ground where slavery did not exist, his status as a slave dissolved, and he should be a free man (instead of being returned, as he had been, as a slave to Missouri). The majority opinion, written by a pro-slavery chief justice, Roger B. Taney, and backed by four other Southern justices on the court, dismissed Scott's appeal as moot. Blacks were never intended by the Constitution to qualify for citizenship, Taney declared, and so Scott had no legal standing to sue in a federal court. But Taney took the additional step of adding that Scott's appeal was intrinsically meritless, because neither Congress nor legislatures in the territories had the power to deprive slaveholders of a right to their slave property. What the Dred Scott decision did, quite deliberately, was to rule any form of popular referendum on slavery—whether in Congress or in the territories themselves—null and void.

Douglas adroitly sidestepped the Dred Scott decision by insisting that popular sovereignty could still work its charms, provided it was done passively—by territorial legislatures and constitutional conventions refusing to adopt the necessary apparatus of slave codes and fugitive slave laws that buttressed slaveholding in the South. But this was straining at the ultimate gnat; and anyway, it was not the conclusion that the newly inaugurated president,

James Buchanan, wanted to endorse as Democratic party orthodoxy. Although Buchanan was a Northerner, he was also a Democrat with big political debts to Southern interests and a cold eye of rivalry toward Stephen Douglas. Buchanan cheerfully hailed the Dred Scott decision as the new law of the land, and he pressed ahead with recommendations to Congress asking for the full admission of Kansas as a state with a pro-slavery constitution drawn up by the pro-slavery Kansas legislature meeting in the town of Lecompton.

Douglas saw at once that if he acquiesced in approving the Lecompton Constitution, his political stock in free-soil Illinois would drop below worthless. But if he opposed the Lecompton Constitution, James Buchanan would grinningly turn every political gun in the Democratic party on him and destroy him. Since his Senate seat in Illinois was up for reelection in 1858, Douglas had no very easy choice. But he needed Illinois more than he needed Buchanan. When Congress convened in December 1857, Douglas broke with Buchanan, fought the acceptance of the Lecompton Constitution until it failed on a technicality, and returned to Illinois in July 1858, praying that Illinois Democrats would resist the demands of James Buchanan that they bury him.

The Lincoln-Douglas Debates

Abraham Lincoln had known Stephen A. Douglas since the 1830s, when both had sat in the Illinois state legislature. Lincoln had not cared much for Douglas then—he snorted that the five-foot-four-inch Douglas was "the least man I ever saw"—and discovered nothing over time that improved the impression. Douglas "will tell a lie to ten thousand people one day, even though he knows he may have to deny it to five thousand the next," Lincoln complained. Nevertheless, Douglas's brass had earned him the political rewards Lincoln had always coveted. "Twenty-two years ago Judge Douglas and I first became acquainted," Lincoln wrote in 1856, "With me, the race of ambition has been a failure—a flat

6. Stephen Arnold Douglas, Democratic Senator from Illinois, 1847–1861.

failure; with him it has been one of splendid success. His name fills the nation; and is not unknown, even, in foreign lands."

The principal reason for Douglas's success, apart from his own personal political charisma, was the solid loyalty of Illinois to the Democratic party, from the time of its admission to the Union in

1818. Only a handful of counties stretching across the middle of the state and up the Illinois River had ever consistently voted Whig. (Lincoln's election to Congress as a Whig in 1847 had been from the congressional district dominated by this "Whig Belt.") But through the 1850s, the thinly settled northern counties of the state exploded with immigrants from the Northeast, and in 1856, when the infant Republican party ran its first presidential candidate, thirty-five of the northernmost Illinois counties went Republican and shifted the balance of Illinois' nine-man Congressional delegation to five Democrat and four Republican. Since the Buchanan-Douglas feud promised to cleave Democratic unity to splinters, Lincoln would probably have no better opportunity to gain the Senate seat he had missed in 1855, and no better opportunity to humiliate the "Little Giant," than in 1858.

First, though, Lincoln needed to make certain that the ungainly collection of anti-Douglas Democrats and ex-Whigs who made up the Illinois Republican party would unite behind him, and in June, the state Republican Committee (chaired by the determined anti-Douglas Democrat, Norman B. Judd) called for a statewide Republican convention to endorse Lincoln. And to raise the stakes still higher, Lincoln devoted his acceptance speech at the convention—which became celebrated as the "House Divided" speech—to drawing the line between himself and Douglas as thickly and brightly as possible.

"We are now far into the fifth year, since a policy was initiated"—namely, the Kansas-Nebraska Act—"with the avowed object, and confident promise, of putting an end to slavery agitation," Lincoln proclaimed. But the results had been entirely the opposite: "Under the operation of that policy, that agitation has not only, not ceased, but has constantly augmented." And so long as Douglas attempted to use the popular sovereignty doctrine to wallpaper-over the real issue, then the controversy and the bloodshed "will not cease, until a crisis shall have been reached, and passed." That real issue was slavery itself, and slavery would keep on dividing the republic because there was no way to reconcile slavery and freedom, or slaveholders and those who hated slavery. "A house divided against itself cannot stand," Lincoln intoned prophetically. "I believe this government cannot endure, permanently half slave and half free." The question, then, was not whether the slavery issue could be charmed away by Douglas's popular-sovereignty wand, but whether the American people were going to make up their minds to either embrace slavery or extinguish it. "Either the opponents of slavery, will arrest the further spread of it, and place it where the public mind shall rest in the belief that it is in course of ultimate extinction; or its advocates will push it forward, till it shall become alike lawful in all the States, old as well as new—North as well as South."

Lincoln did not mean that the divided halves would need to resort to violence to resolve the division; what *was* needed, though, was a national decision that slavery was right or wrong, and then the taking of whatever gradual steps were consistent with that conclusion, especially concerning the territories. If slavery was wrong, then there was no point to popular sovereignty, and Douglas's arguments were bankrupt. On the other hand, an argument supporting popular sovereignty, even in its passive Douglasite form, suggested that Douglas believed slavery was, at least, morally acceptable. And so Lincoln turned on Douglas and broadly suggested that Douglas's popular sovereignty and the Dred Scott decision were in fact part of larger strategy, confected by Buchanan, Taney, and Douglas, "to educate and mould public opinion, at least Northern public opinion, to not care whether slavery is voted down or voted up." The "squabble … between the President and the author of the Nebraska bill" over "the Lecompton constitution" was purely a matter of appearances.

Douglas began his own campaign on July 9 in Chicago, denying that a division of national opinion over slavery posed any threat at all to the national house: "Our complex system of State and Federal Government contemplated diversity and dissimilarity in the local institutions of each and every State then in the Union." Why, then, should a "dissimilarity" between the states over slavery bother anyone, especially when the bother concerned the status of mere Negroes? "This government of ours is founded on the white basis," and has no need to pick at its conscience over what happened to blacks. But Lincoln and the Republicans wanted to put blacks on "an equality with the white race," and to get that equality, Lincoln would risk "a war of the sections—a war of the North against the South—of the free States against the slave States—a war of extermination . . . until . . . all the States shall either become free or become slave."

From that point, Douglas proceeded to behave as though Lincoln was beneath any further notice, and he began a triumphant reelection parade through central Illinois. The hostile pressure of Buchanan cost a number of prominent Douglasites their political jobs; but to Buchanan's rage, Illinois Democrats largely stayed loyal to Douglas. Meanwhile, Lincoln's underfunded campaign was left to hop pathetically along after Douglas from meeting to meeting, hoping for the chance to speak after Douglas to the crowds Douglas had gathered. This only made Lincoln look ridiculous, and at the end of July, with prodding from Norman Judd, Lincoln challenged Douglas to a series of open-air debates. Douglas had no need to accept the challenge. Why should he agree to share time with Lincoln as an equal? But after some initial hesitation, Douglas decided that debating would only speed up the process of felling Lincoln, and he named seven locations in Illinois where neither of them had as yet made speeches.

This turned out to be the greatest miscalculation of Douglas's life, since the debates not only gave Lincoln a place in direct sight of the voters, but opened Douglas to solo verbal combat with someone who had spent a lifetime honing his skills of cut and thrust. And over the course of the seven debates, from August 21 to

October 15, Douglas had ample reason to regret his decision. His primary weapons against Lincoln were smears: Lincoln was a closet abolitionist who was trying to lure moderate Republicans and old-line Whigs into supporting a radical anti-slavery agenda...Lincoln was a race-mixer who wanted to make the freed slaves every white man's equal and every white woman's lover...Lincoln wanted to make war on the Supreme Court and on the South, "to agitate this country, to array the North against the South, and convert us into enemies instead of friends."

Lincoln denied that he was promoting any of these bugaboos. For one thing, as Lincoln had been arguing since 1854, there was a big difference between talking about the civil or social rights of black people, and then denying, as slavery did, that blacks also lacked any natural rights, especially the natural rights promised to everyone in the Declaration of Independence, to life, liberty, and the pursuit of happiness.

> There is no reason in the world why the negro is not entitled to all the natural rights enumerated in the Declaration of Independence, the right to life, liberty and the pursuit of happiness. I hold that he is as much entitled to these as the white man. I agree with Judge Douglas he is not my equal in many respects....But in the right to eat the bread, without leave of anybody else, which his own hand earns, he is my equal and the equal of Judge Douglas, and the equal of every living man.

The natural equality of blacks and whites meant that the enslavement of blacks could not be merely a matter of political indifference that white Illinoisans could leave up to popular sovereignty in the territories; taking away one man's natural rights could just as easily become a threat to the natural rights of everyone else. "Judge Douglas," Lincoln declared, "and whoever like him teaches that the negro has no share, humble though it may be, in the Declaration of Independence, is going back to the era of our liberty and independence, and...he is penetrating, so far as lies in his power, the human soul, and eradicating the light of reason and the love of liberty, when he is in every possible way preparing the public mind, by his vast influence, for making the institution of slavery perpetual." It was time Illinoisans realized that Douglas's race card, like all race cards, was really a license to destroy the basic principle of liberty itself. Lincoln said,

> That is the real issue. That is the issue that will continue in this country when these poor tongues of Judge Douglas and myself shall be silent. It is the eternal struggle between these two principles— right and wrong—throughout the world. They are the two principles that have stood face to face from the beginning of time; and will ever continue to struggle. The one is the common right of humanity and the other the divine right of kings. It is the same principle in whatever shape it develops itself. It is the same spirit that says, "You work and toil and earn bread, and I'll eat it." No matter in what shape it comes, whether from the mouth of a king who seeks to bestride the people of his own nation and live by the fruit of their labor, or from one race of men as an apology for enslaving another race, it is the same tyrannical principle.

For Douglas, the problem with the slavery controversy was that it was a controversy, and popular sovereignty was the means for dampening controversy. When Lincoln "tells you that I will not argue the question whether slavery is right or wrong," Lincoln is perfectly correct: "I hold that under the Constitution of the United States, each State of this Union has a right to do as it pleases on the subject of slavery." For Lincoln, however, the slavery controversy was about slavery, and anything that did less than look slavery plainly in the eye as a violation of natural law would never dampen anything. Lincoln was not asking people to be "so impatient of it as a wrong as to disregard its actual presence among us and the difficulty of getting rid of it suddenly in a satisfactory way, and to disregard the constitutional obligations thrown about it." But understanding that slavery *is* a moral wrong should convince people to desire its "ultimate extinction," something which was not going to be achieved by giving it a toss of the coin in the territories through popular sovereignty.

Unhappily, the Lincoln-Douglas debates, unlike a boxing match or even a modern Oxford-style collegiate debate, had no point system. The only way to measure how well the candidates had done would be in the fall elections and even that would be difficult to determine, since (as in 1855) elections to the U.S. Senate would be carried out by the state legislature in January 1859. If Illinois voters were consciously voting for legislative candidates in November 1858, who would, in turn, vote for Lincoln or Douglas, and doing so on the basis of the performances of each in the debates, then we would have to say that Lincoln should have won. Republican candidates for the lower House of the state legislature garnered 190,468 votes to 166,374 for Democratic candidates; Republican candidates for the state Senate polled 53,784 votes, while 44,750 went to Democratic candidates. Taken just on the aggregate numbers, Illinois Republicans won a robust 54 percent of the vote.

The problem was that they won it unevenly. The apportionment of representation in the legislature had not been adjusted since 1854, and older downstate (and Democratic) districts still elected more representatives per capita than those representing the rapidly expanding Republican districts in the north. "If the State had been apportioned according to population," complained Joseph Medill, the editor of the *Chicago Tribune*, "the districts carried by the Republicans would have returned forty-one Lincoln representatives, and fourteen Lincoln Senators, which of course would have elected him." But the actual returns sent fifty-four Democratic legislators back to the state capitol in Springfield, and only forty-six Republicans. And on January 5, 1859, when the legislature cast its votes for U.S. Senator, the balloting went strictly down party lines and reelected Douglas. "It hurts too much to laugh," Lincoln admitted, "and I am too big to cry."

And yet, the great debates had been far from merely another political disappointment for Lincoln. He had come within an ace of upsetting the most famous and powerful Democrat in Congress, and he had done so on the back of a series of debates whose transcripts, recorded by teams of shorthand-trained reporters hired by the principal Illinois newspapers, were picked up and printed across the North. "Mr. Lincoln is a man of very great ability; few men in the nation would willingly encounter him in debate," wrote the *National Era* two weeks after the election. "We have heard many men in all parts of the Union, and think, for clear statement, the simplifying of difficult points, taking into consideration his rectitude and singleness of purpose, he is our choice." A political operative from Pennsylvania told Lincoln, "Seriously, Lincoln, Judge Douglas being so widely know, you are getting national reputation.... Your discussion with Judge Douglas had demonstrated your ability and your devotion to freedom; you have no embarrassing record; you have sprung from the humble walks of life, sharing in its toils and trials; and if only we can get these facts sufficiently before the people, depend on it, there is some chance for you." Already, Northerners were beginning to speak of Lincoln as an ideal Republican candidate—not for the Senate, but for president of the United States. "Let me assure you," wrote the *Chicago Tribune*'s Horace White, who had covered the debates as a reporter, "Your popular majority in the state will give us the privilege of naming our man on the national ticket in 1860."

Election to the presidency, 1860

No one thought such political dreams more unlikely than Abraham Lincoln. He had become, in his own eyes, a perennial loser, and in the future he expected that "I shall fight in the ranks," or perhaps even "sink out of view, and shall be Forgotten." The notion that he was presidential material, especially after the loss to Douglas, seemed risible. "Just think of such a sucker as me as president!" he exclaimed to the journalist, Henry Villard. And yet, feelers about his interest in a presidential nomination kept arriving in the mail. "I must, in candor, say I do not think myself fit for the Presidency," he told one overeager newspaper editor, even though "I certainly am flattered, and gratified, that some partial friends think of me in that connection." By early 1859 he was beginning to get invitations to appear before Republican meetings and conventions in Boston, Iowa, Minnesota, Ohio, Indiana, Wisconsin, and even the Kansas territory, as well as proposals from publishers to issue the debates as a book.

Lincoln took every opportunity offered by these events to pummel Douglas and popular sovereignty anew, especially since Douglas, fresh from his vindication in Illinois, was the agreed-upon front-runner for the Democratic presidential nomination in 1860. In the process, Lincoln also unfolded a liberal alternative to the reactionary political economy of Douglas and the Democrats. In the Democratic imagination, the ideal world was one of static relationships between classes. On the bottom, providing the most basic but demeaning forms of labor, was a class of slaves, marked and fixed by their color; in the middle were independent farmers and urban workers whose discontents were salved by generous subsidies (in the form of cheap foreign imports); at the top were great but beneficent landowners, playing the Jeffersonian role of an indulgent republican oligarchy.

For this, Lincoln had precisely the same contempt Cobden and Bright had for the Corn Law aristocrats. "The just and generous, and prosperous system," Lincoln said, is the dynamic one, the path of middle-class aspiration "which opens the way for all—gives hope to all, and energy, and progress, and improvement of condition to all." It had been his experience that "the prudent, penniless beginner in the world, labors for wages awhile, saves a surplus with which to buy tools or land, for himself; then labors on his own account another while, and at length hires another new beginner to help him." He wanted no world of Jeffersonian grandees, offering farmers and the working class the anesthetic of freely available slave labor in order to lull them into contentment with their lot. What he wanted was opportunity and mobility, not subsidy and stasis, and he was "asking no favors of capital on the one hand, nor of hirelings or slaves on the other." It was the glory of a free-labor system that "that there is no such thing as a freeman being fatally fixed for life, in the condition of a hired laborer." And he had all of Cobden and Bright's confidence that the tide of progress was flowing in the liberal direction. "I have an abiding faith that we shall beat them in the long run," he wrote, "As there is a just and righteous God in Heaven, our principles will and shall prevail sooner or later."

The most telling opportunity to explain himself came in mid-October 1859, from James A. Briggs, on behalf of the Young Men's Central Republican Union of New York City, to speak "on any subject you please" in February. Lincoln was to give one in a series of lectures by prominent "western" Republicans (the list included Frank P. Blair of Missouri and Cassius M. Clay of Kentucky), but there was little doubt that an invitation to speak in New York City had the ultimate purpose allowing the East Coast Republican leadership a chance to size him up as a potential national candidate.

Along with the New York invitation, however, the continuing national argument over slavery rose up to cast a new and more grotesque shadow. On October 16, grizzled old John Brown, the iron man of the Pottawattomie massacre in Kansas, launched a raid on the federal arsenal at Harpers Ferry, Virginia, intent on seizing weapons with which to arm a slave uprising. The raid fizzled into a bloody failure, and Brown was tried for treason (against the Commonwealth of Virginia) and hanged on December 2. But the raid sent cyclones of panic through the slaveholding South, especially when investigations of Brown's supporters revealed that the raid had been financed by a group of wealthy Northern abolitionists. Appalled at such "malignant hostility," Southern newspapers and journals howled that Brown was only "the vanguard of the great army intended for our subjugation," while in Congress, Southern senators promised that "the South will demand" that the Democratic party abandon any hope that popular sovereignty would keep the territories open for slavery by "explicitly declaring that slave property is entitled in the Territories and on the high seas to the same protection that is given to any other and every other species of property." The South must have free access to the territories; Northern anti-slavery societies must be outlawed; laws for recovering runaway slaves must be enforced; and the Constitution must be amended to deprive the federal government of any authority to touch slavery. Otherwise, Southern Democrats would withdraw from the party and nominate their own candidate.

The radicalization of Southern opinion was political death to Stephen A. Douglas, who knew he could not, after the Brown raid, appease both the Northern and Southern wings of the party, but who was certainly not going to surrender his presidential ambitions in favor of some Southern fire-eater who would probably lose the Northern Democratic vote and throw the presidential election to the Republicans. It was a political godsend, however, for Abraham Lincoln. Up until the beginning of 1860, the betting money on the Republican presidential nomination was resting on either New York senator William Henry Seward or Ohio governor Salmon Portland Chase. Both Seward and Chase had long connections with abolitionism in their political baggage— which seemed unproblematic, so long as the Republicans were the minority party and felt it was more important to make an ideological statement with a nominee than try to win an election. But if the Democratic party split, and the factions ran opposing candidates and divided the national Democratic vote, then a Republican might be the winner after all, if only by default. And so it behooved the Republican leadership in 1860 to think about offering a presidential candidate who was more moderate, and more electable, than pure.

Positioning himself as precisely that electable moderate became Lincoln's strategy in his speech for the Young Men's Central Republican Union. Speaking to a capacity audience in the Great Hall of the new Cooper Institute on February 27, 1860, Lincoln assured his audience that the only issue he was concerned with was whether "anything in the Constitution, forbade the Federal Government, to control as to slavery in federal territory." If it did, both popular sovereignty and the Dred Scott dictum would disappear, and the way would be open for Congress to reassert responsibility for the status of slavery in the territories; but that did not mean that he had any interest in attacking slavery in the Southern states, where state sovereignty immunized slavery from federal control. "No Republican designedly aided or encouraged the Harper's [*sic*] Ferry affair," Lincoln asserted. In fact, his advice to Republicans was, "even though the southern people will not so much as listen to us, let us calmly consider their demands, and yield to them if, in our deliberate view of our duty, we possibly can." What Republicans should not yield, however, is the conviction that slavery is a moral wrong. They could, he repeated, "afford to let it alone where it is, because that much is due to the necessity arising from its actual presence in the nation"; but that fundamental belief in the immorality of slavery also meant that Republicans could not allow slavery to expand further, as though it contained no offence at all, "to spread into the National Territories, and to overrun us here in these Free States." And he brought the Great Hall to its feet with the rousing charge:
LET US HAVE FAITH THAT RIGHT MAKES MIGHT, AND IN THAT FAITH, LET US, TO THE END, DARE TO DO OUR DUTY AS WE UNDERSTAND IT.

Meanwhile, in Illinois, Norman Judd was eager to make up for Lincoln's loss to Douglas in the 1858 Senate race, and in order to position Lincoln for at least a favorite-son nomination, Judd persuaded the Republican national committee to hold its national nominating convention in Chicago in May 1860. Armed with the Cooper Institute speech, and with the argument that nominating Chase or Seward would jeopardize the chance of

7. Abraham Lincoln, photographed at Mathew Brady's studio before delivering his Cooper Union address, February 27, 1860.

winning a Republican victory, Lincoln's backers secured a state-wide endorsement of Lincoln for the presidency at the Illinois state Republican convention on May 6 (where his cousin, John Hanks, introduced him as the "Rail Splitter," bringing along a few fence rails, which Hanks claimed he and Lincoln had split back in 1830). Ten days later, Judd and the Illinois Republican delegates steamed into the Chicago convention, warning that Lincoln was the only candidate with any hope of binding moderates and anti-slavery Democrats to the Republican platform. To the dismay of William Seward's campaign staff, who had expected the convention to be the New Yorker's political coronation, the convention opened with Lincoln in second place in the delegate balloting. After two more ballots, Lincoln had bested Seward and won the Republican presidential nomination.

The election that November came almost as an anticlimax. Predictably, the Southern Democrats would no longer regard Douglas and popular sovereignty as sufficient guarantees for slavery, and they bolted the Democratic national convention to nominate a Kentuckian, John C. Breckinridge, for president. Douglas was duly nominated by the rump of the Democratic convention, but even as they did so, they knew that neither half of a divided Democratic vote could stop a unified Republican one, especially as it gathered around a candidate who professed only moderation and declined to do any public campaigning where he could be tricked into committing some political faux pas on slavery. On Election Day, November 6, 1860, Lincoln polled only 1.9 million votes, and Breckinridge and Douglas came in with 2 million. But with that slight edge hopelessly split between Douglas and Breckinridge, Lincoln was left the winner in both popular voting and the electoral college (where he outran his competitors by 180 to 123).

The Southern states wasted no time in disclosing their response: if Douglas and popular sovereignty were no longer acceptable,

the prospect of an anti-slavery Republican as president was
even less so. "Lincoln's election," wailed South Carolina senator
James Chestnut, is nothing else than "a decree for emancipation.
Slavery cannot survive four years of an administration whose
overwhelming influences" were hostile to slavery's health.
Three days later, on November 9, the South Carolina
legislature took the first step and called for the election of a
state convention to consider seceding from the Federal Union.

Chapter 6
Emancipation

The secession crisis and Fort Sumter

Secession is not an easy doctrine to follow. Strictly speaking, it meant only that individual member states of the American Union had concluded to go their own way, with no more ado than resigning from a club. But the Union was a nation, not a club, and it had been becoming more of a nation all through the nineteenth century. Secession, in order to be convincing, had to be fueled by darker energies than mere disagreement, and foremost among those energies was slavery. No matter how much Southerners squirmed to admit it (and it is shocking in retrospect to learn how many of them did no squirming at all about acknowledging "African slavery as it exists among us" as the "cornerstone" of Southern resistance), it was the self-interest invested in human bondage that nerved the hands of the disunionists. Secession also gained plausibility from geography, because all of the slave states lay in great southern bloc, contiguous to each other, and if they all acted together, they could take on the lineaments of a real nation of their own.

Even so, secession from the Union still seemed a terrible form of brinkmanship. South Carolina bolted ahead on December 20, 1860, announcing that it was withdrawing from the Union, followed by Mississippi, Alabama, Florida, Georgia, Louisiana, and Texas. But then the rush stopped. Virginia, North Carolina, Tennessee, Arkansas, Maryland, Kentucky, and Missouri—all slave states along the upper tier of slave South—showed little inclination to applaud secession. Without them, and especially without Virginia, a secession movement had small chance of success, and Lincoln intended to do everything in his power to ensure that they had no occasion to wish themselves partners with their lower South sisters. Even there, he believed that secession was probably more bluff than substance, and a little forbearance on his part might give loyalists there the chance to turn the political tables. He refused to make any statement of how he planned to respond to secession—or at least none in advance of his inauguration in March—and he privately assured as many Southerners as would listen that a Republican president would do nothing to "directly, or indirectly, interfere with their slaves, or with them, about their slaves." Presidents of the United States, after all, possess no imperial powers. Even if he had wanted to eliminate slavery with a wave of his hand, Lincoln knew he could not actually lay that hand on slavery so long as slavery was a matter of individual state enactments and protected by the federal Constitution's firewall between federal and state jurisdictions.

Lincoln reserved to himself only two points: that he would not consent to calling slavery right, and that he would not endorse any further extension of slavery into the territories (which *were* under federal jurisdiction, no matter what the Dred Scott decision claimed). So, on the one hand, he dismissed the seven lower South secessions as temporary political aberrations: "there is no more" behind the secessions "than anxiety, for there is nothing going wrong. It is a consoling circumstance that when we look out there is nothing that really hurts anybody." And on the other, he quietly encouraged his allies in Congress to disregard the secession fever: "my opinion is that no state can, in any way lawfully, get out of the Union, without the consent of the others; and that it is the duty of the

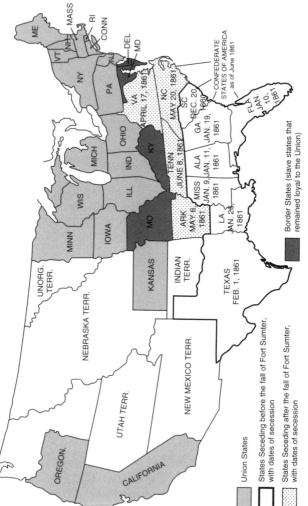

Map 2. Secession and Civil War, 1861.

Union States

States Seceding before the fall of Fort Sumter, with dates of secession

States Seceding after the fall of Fort Sumter, with dates of secession

Border States (slave states that remained loyal to the Union)

VA APRIL 17, 1861

NC MAY 20, 1861

SC DEC. 20, 1860

CONFEDERATE STATES OF AMERICA as of June 1861

FLA JAN. 10, 1861

GA JAN. 19, 1861

ALA JAN. 11, 1861

TENN JUNE 8, 1861

MISS JAN. 9, 1861

ARK MAY 6, 1861

LA JAN. 26, 1861

TEXAS FEB. 1, 1861

INDIAN TERR.

KANSAS

NEBRASKA TERR.

UNORG. TERR.

UTAH TERR.

NEW MEXICO TERR.

OREGON.

CALIFORNIA

MINN

IOWA

WIS

ILL

MICH

IND

OHIO

KY

MO

PA

NY

ME

VT

NH

MASS

RI

CONN

NJ

DEL

MD

President, and other government functionaries to run the machine as it is."

But Lincoln was not seeing what Southerners saw. Lincoln might argue that a president had no authority to lay hands on slavery; but every Southerner knew he could do the next best thing, which was to unsettle it. If "Mr. Lincoln places among us his Judges, District Attorneys, Marshals, Post Masters, Custom House officers, etc.," raged Georgia governor Joseph Brown, he will be able to seduce unsteady Southern whites to create a Southern Republican party, flood "the country with inflammatory Abolition doctrines," and create a climate of fear, which would produce either a slave insurrection or else a hasty abandonment of slavery in order to avoid one. The day of Southern hegemony in American politics was past, and Southerners had no reason to suppose that it would ever come back. "All the powers of a Government which has so long sheltered it will be turned to its destruction," wailed the *Augusta Daily Constitutionalist*. The South's only hope "is out of the Union."

Just how little Lincoln understood this terror can be measured by his refusal to pay attention to the organization of a provisional secessionist supergovernment (to be known as the Confederate States of America) or to the demands of the Confederate States for the surrender of federal property within their boundaries. In most cases, the secessionist state governments simply seized federal property outright, from the federal mint in New Orleans down to a one-gun federal revenue cutter. What posed a greater difficulty were the federal coastal forts that guarded the major ports of the Atlantic coastline, which could not be seized so effortlessly. The chief irritant among those posts was Fort Sumter, sitting on a man-made island in the center of Charleston harbor. To the extent that South Carolina had led the secession pack, the presence of Fort Sumter, sitting athwart the harbor channel of its greatest city, was a symbolic embarrassment, while the refusal of Sumter's commandant,

Major Robert Anderson, to surrender the two small artillery companies that occupied it became a downright provocation.

By Lincoln's reasoning, the longer Sumter held out, the more the Confederates looked hesitant and afraid to challenge federal authority, and the more likely that honeyed words would deflate the secession enthusiasm. At his inauguration on the east front of the Capitol in Washington on March 4, 1861, Lincoln insisted that secession was a legal and constitutional impossibility, that "no State, upon its own mere motion, can lawfully get out of the Union—that resolves and ordinances to that effect are legally void; and that acts of violence, within any State or States, against the authority of the United States, are insurrectionary or revolutionary." Still, "there needs to be no bloodshed or violence...All the vital rights of minorities"—and here he clearly meant the *Southern* minority—"are so plainly assured to them, by affirmations and negations, guaranties and prohibition in the Constitution, that controversies never arise concerning them." Rather than rushing to some illusory refuge out of the Union, Southerners should "think calmly and well, upon this whole subject. Nothing valuable can be lost by taking time." And when they did, they would remember that they are more Americans than Southerners. "The mystic chords of memory, stretching from every battle-field, and patriot grave, to every living heart and hearthstone, all over this broad land, will yet swell the chorus of the Union, when again touched, as surely they will be, by the better angels of our nature."

The next day, it was Lincoln who learned that he might lose a very great deal by taking time. On the morning after his inauguration, the outgoing secretary of war, Joseph Holt, delivered to Lincoln a dispatch from Major Anderson that warned that Anderson had only six weeks' worth of supplies left in Fort Sumter. Once they were gone, his little garrison would have to surrender or starve. This caught Lincoln wholly by surprise, and the surprise became more pointed as Lincoln realized that the army

8. Inauguration of Abraham Lincoln as sixteenth president, March 4, 1861.

and navy were too small and too unprepared to fight their way to Anderson's defense. For three weeks Lincoln twisted this way and that, soliciting advice from his cabinet, sounding out representatives from the upper South states, struggling to determine whether an attack on Sumter by the Confederates would drive the upper South to denounce the secession radicals or pull it into the secession vortex. Finally, at the end of March, he offered a compromise to the Confederates: he would send relief ships to Sumter, but they would be unarmed (except for their escorts) and carry only food and medicine. "If such attempt be not resisted," Lincoln promised the governor of South Carolina, Francis Pickens, "no effort to throw in men, arms, or ammunition, will be made, without further notice."

This seemingly artless suggestion startled the new Confederate government and its provisional president, Jefferson Davis, into a frenzy of alarm. The Confederates could not let Sumter be resupplied, because that would only prolong the status quo and grant Lincoln extra innings to sap the momentum of secession. Davis authorized the commander of the Confederate batteries surrounding Charleston harbor to demand an immediate surrender. Major Anderson refused, and at 4:30 on the morning of April 12, the Confederate guns began battering Sumter's three-story brick walls. Forty-eight hours later, Anderson agreed to surrender—not because the Confederates had done any serious damage to Sumter (in fact, not a single man of his garrison had been killed by the Confederate bombardment), but because he had finally come to the end of his supplies.

If Lincoln hoped that the Confederate attack on Sumter would shock the upper South into denouncing secession as a game that had gone too far, he could not have been more wrong. The day after Sumter surrendered, Lincoln issued a proclamation, declaring the secessionist state governments to be in unlawful rebellion, leaving him "no choice...but to call out the war power of the Government." Following the letter of the federal Militia Act of 1795, Lincoln called on the rest of the states to put 75,000 of their state militia at his disposal "to maintain the honor, the integrity, and the existence of our National Union, and the perpetuity of popular government." To his dismay, the upper South flatly refused. "Kentucky will furnish no troops for the wicked purpose of subduing her sister Southern States," replied Kentucky's governor, Beriah Magoffin. The upper South had not voted for Lincoln, and they were disinclined to step off the sidelines on Lincoln's behalf. Even more, they feared that any Lincolnite militia marching over their fields and mountains to deal with the secessionists of the lower South might touch off exactly the slave insurrections John Brown had dreamed of; or worse, be used deliberately as an engine to compel the emancipation their own slaves.

Faced with a choice between cooperating in their own self-destruction, and cooperating with the secessionists, most of the upper South would take its chances beside the secessionists. On April 16 Virginia voted to secede, followed by Tennessee, Arkansas, and North Carolina; on April 19, secessionist mobs rioted in the streets of Baltimore when the first militia units from Massachusetts tried to pass through the city on the way to Washington. Only adroit maneuvering by federal officers in Missouri and Maryland, and a hesitant legislature in Kentucky, kept them from joining the new secession stampede and advancing the Confederacy's border to the Potomac and Ohio rivers.

Lincoln tried to assure whatever Southerners were still listening that he intended to use the militia only for restoring federal authority in the lower South, not for tampering with slavery. And if the militia could be formed without delay into a strike force that would boldly march straight at the new Confederate government (which had, conveniently for Lincoln's purposes, established itself only one hundred miles from Washington, in Richmond, Virginia) and knock it backwards with a sudden Andrew Jackson-like blow, the vast majority of Southerners might still be shocked back into their loyal senses, and the hastily constructed Confederate regime would fall in on itself. Unhappily, it took until July to assemble and sort out the chaotic jumble of ill-trained soldier-volunteers who rallied to his call, and when 35,000 of them lumbered haphazardly down the road to Richmond, they collided with a Confederate army of more-or-less equal size and unpreparedness just above Manassas Junction. The overconfident Union troops were thrown into confusion, and ended the fight in a disorganized run to the safety of Washington. After only four months, the Lincoln presidency looked like nothing but a string of miscalculations, and the Confederacy looked as though it had achieved the unthinkable with almost insolent ease.

Democracy and emancipation

The battle of Manassas (or Bull Run, as it was also called from the stream the Confederates had used as a defensive line) was a staggering blow to the assumption that with one firm swipe of the federal hand, the Confederacy would collapse in repentant jibbers. Opinion, therefore, promptly swung from unfounded optimism to unfounded pessimism. In Richmond, the newspapers crowed that "It is no longer doubtful whether we can maintain our ground against the foe." The only question was when the Confederacy would "have an army in the field large enough to command the city of Washington; and shall dictate from there the terms on which we shall treat with the North." On the Northern end, Horace Greeley sweatily asked Lincoln, "Can the Rebels be beaten after all that has occurred?" An "Armistice for thirty, sixty, ninety, 120 days—better still, for a year—ought at once to be proposed with a view to a peaceful adjustment." On every brow, Greeley moaned, "sits sullen, scowling, black despair."

Not on Lincoln's brow, though. Lincoln was temperamentally unflappable, almost to the point of appearing passive, and moreover he was possessed of liberalism's secular confidence that the arc of history pointed toward liberty and democracy, not toward a reactionary throwback regime of slaveholders. He called for the recruitment of a new, expanded army of three-year volunteers, and selected as their generalissimo a dashing and multitalented West Pointer from one of Philadelphia's first families, George Brinton McClellan. And rather than fumbling to minimize the secession mess, Lincoln actually raised its stakes. In his welcoming address to a specially called meeting of Congress in July, Lincoln abandoned any pretense that secession was simply Southern political bluff; he had learned the hard way that its dangers were very real indeed, and those dangers pointed a dagger at the very heart of liberal democracy.

"This issue embraces more than the fate of these United States," Lincoln warned. "It presents to the whole family of man, the question, whether a constitutional republic, or a democracy—a government of the people, by the same people—" is doomed by the very popular consent upon which it is built. The essence of liberal democracy, Lincoln had said in 1854, was that "no man is good enough to govern another man, without that other's consent." But part of that consent was the mutual agreement that once a majority of citizens had decided upon a course of action, those who had not consented to the specific action nevertheless still consented to the legitimacy of the majority's rule. Secession was the diametric opposite of this spirit—and a demonstration that popular government on the liberal model was inherently unworkable. Secession "presents the question, whether discontented individuals . . . can always . . . and thus practically put an end to free government upon the earth." Looking back on the defeat of European liberalism only a decade and a half before, secession in the United States now "forces us to ask: 'Is there, in all republics, this inherent, and fatal weakness?' " Are all liberal democracies inherently unstable? "So viewing the issue" of secession as a challenge to the very principle of liberal democracy, "no choice was left but to call out the war power of the Government." And no choice would be left but to fight the secessionists to the finish and restore the Union.

Above all, rather than continuing to downplay the Republican project to contain and extinguish slavery, Lincoln began tinkering with plans to promote emancipation in the upper South's "border states"—the key slave states along the Ohio and Potomac rivers that had remained loyal to the Union—Delaware, Maryland, Kentucky, and Missouri. From the first day of the war, radical Republicans in Congress had badgered Lincoln to use the secession crisis as a pretext for decreeing the emancipation of all the South's slaves and destroying the whole slavery problem at one stroke. "Under the war power," declared Massachusetts senator Charles

Sumner in Lincoln's office the day the news of the Sumter attack arrived, "the right had come to him to emancipate the slaves." In practical terms, this would derange the Confederacy's ability to muster its slave-labor force for military purposes; in political terms, it would convert the war into a liberal crusade to break the back of the Southern agrarian oligarchs.

It would also, as Lincoln patiently replied, be unconstitutional. Presidents had no constitutional power to overturn any state's slavery statutes merely by proclamation. And there was always the chance that any direct movement against slavery in the border states might reignite the secession fire and stampede the border states into the hands of the Confederates. And that said nothing about the problems posed by what to do with the freed slaves the day afterward . . . what the legal consequences might be if slaveholders challenged an emancipation decree in a federal court system with Roger Taney (of *Dred Scott* ill-fame) still at its head . . . or what case he could still make for liberal democracy if he began ruling by proclamation. When the commandant of the Department of Missouri, John Charles Frémont, issued his own emancipation decree, based on the power of martial law, Lincoln revoked it and later relieved Frémont of command.

There was no jurisprudence in American law that established what the martial-law powers of generals or presidents were, and emancipation did not look like the issue with which to begin that determination. "Can it be pretended that it is any longer the government of the U.S . . . wherein a General, or a President, may make permanent rules of property by proclamation?" Lincoln asked after canceling Frémont's proclamation. "No doubt the thing was popular in some quarters," he admitted, but "Kentucky would be turned against us," and "to lose Kentucky is nearly the same as to lose the whole game. Kentucky gone, we can not hold Missouri, nor, as I think, Maryland. These all against us, and the job on our hands is too large for us. We would as well consent to separation at once, including the surrender of this capitol."

That did not mean, however, that Lincoln had lost interest in emancipation, or that he did not have more subtle ways than war-powers proclamations to effect it. For one thing, Lincoln's incessant disclaimers throughout 1861 that the war was being fought for the preservation of the Union rather than for emancipation disguised in plain sight the fact that restoring the Union *was* the ultimate means of ending slavery. The Confederates had seceded precisely to avoid being coerced into emancipation; and bringing them back into the Union was the only way to restore the federal jurisdiction that could provide coercion. Without a restored Union, Lincoln had no more power to emancipate the South's slaves than he had for emancipating Spanish Cuba's.

Moreover, if there were uncertainties about emancipation by proclamation (and there were), such uncertainties would disappear if he could persuade slaveholders to emancipate their slaves themselves. By the fall of 1861 Lincoln had drafted an emancipation plan for the Delaware state legislature that looked to free all children born to Delaware slaves after the plan's adoption date, and all other slaves over the age of thirty-five; all others would become free when they arrived at age thirty-five. The sweetener that would induce Delaware slaveholders to embrace this plan was a Congressional authorization to pay the state of Delaware $719,200 in 6 percent United States bonds, doled out in thirty-one annual installments. If they preferred to accelerate the timetable, the compensation could be compressed into ten payments of $71,920, which would completely eliminate slavery in Delaware by 1872.

Lincoln believed that the success of the Delaware proposition could "be made use of as the initiative to hitch the whole thing to." Delaware emancipation would create a domino effect that would allow the same pressure to be laid on Kentucky, Missouri, and Maryland; and once the impetus of legislative emancipation began, the Confederates, staking their hopes for success on wooing the border states into rebellion, would collapse in dismay. Above all, let Congress and the state legislatures cooperate in the plan, and there would be no grounds for dangerous appeals to the federal court system. "If Congress will pass a law authorizing the issuance of bonds for the payment of the emancipated Negroes in the border states, Delaware, Maryland, Kentucky, and Missouri will accept the terms the passage," Lincoln predicted. By these means, "it seemed to him that gradual emancipation and governmental compensation" would bring slavery "to an end."

The limits of liberal democracy

Lincoln's plan might have had a plausible chance of killing both the bird of secession and the bird of slavery with a single stone, had it not been for two unanticipated difficulties. The first was with his armies. After a brief flush of military successes along the Atlantic coastline (the capture of the Hatteras Sound and the Carolina Sea Islands) and the river systems of the West (the swift seizure of Forts Henry and Donelson in western Tennessee, which compelled Confederate troops to abandon their hold on most of Tennessee and Kentucky), the federal armies sank into checkmate.

A worse checkmate was suffered by George Brinton McClellan, the "Young Napoleon." McClellan was strictly opposed to emancipation, and he crossed Lincoln's demands for a renewed march on Richmond with an indirect plan to land Union forces below Richmond on the James River Peninsula. Lincoln tolerated McClellan's resistance. "Little Mac" was an undeniably talented organizer, and his plan to use the federal navy's command of the coastal waters to land his troops on the Peninsula, within a few days' march of Richmond rather than slogging overland, embodied the most advanced strategic ideas of the century. But once McClellan's army landed on the Peninsula, McClellan moved with agonizing slowness; and once the Confederate army (under Robert E. Lee) took advantage of that slowness and launched its own counterblows, McClellan retreated, howling that Lincoln had deliberately denied him reinforcements in order to insure his fall. And when, at the beginning of July 1862, Lincoln came down personally to McClellan's encampment on the James River at Harrison's Landing, McClellan brazenly informed him that unless Lincoln handed over complete control of military operations and abandoned any plans to promote emancipation, McClellan's army would not fight. "A declaration of radical views, especially upon slavery," threatened McClellan, "will rapidly disintegrate our armies."

But the worst checkmate of all was political. Lincoln's "Act for the Gradual Emancipation of Slaves in the State of Delaware" narrowly failed adoption by the Delaware legislature in February 1862; taking the narrowness of the failure as a promising sign, Lincoln recommended broadening the act's offer "to co-operate with any state which may adopt gradual abolishment of slavery" of the act to all four border states. But the border states' representatives in Congress rose up as one to assure Lincoln that they would never cooperate with any such plan. Lincoln's plan, they replied, was "the most extraordinary resolution that was ever introduced into an American Congress; extraordinary in its origin" and "mischievous in its tendency." In "what clause of the Constitution," they asked indignantly, does Lincoln find "the power in Congress to appropriate the treasury of the United States to buy negroes, or to set them free"?

Caught between the obduracy of the border states and the thinly veiled military threat of McClellan, Lincoln found himself running out of possibilities both for restoring the Union *and* for emancipation. But as many a courtroom opponent could have testified, painting Abraham Lincoln into corners was an exceedingly difficult thing to do. Within a week of returning from Harrison's Landing, Lincoln had decided to turn to the idea of a military-style proclamation of emancipation, based on his war powers as commander in chief. This was, as Secretary of the Navy Gideon Welles wrote in his diary, "a new departure for the President, for until this time ... he had been prompt and emphatic in denouncing any interference by the General Government with the subject." But now, "a change of policy in the conduct of the war was necessary." On July 22, 1862, Lincoln read to his cabinet the draft of an emancipation proclamation, based on his presidential war powers, which declared the slaves of the rebels "thenceforward, and forever free." He was conscious of being on thin legal ice by invoking his war powers, and so he was careful to justify the proclamation "as a fit and necessary military measure ... to suppress insurrection," and to limit its application only to the secessionist states (and even then, *not* to those portions of the Confederacy under Union occupation).

Lincoln may have been ready to issue his emancipation proclamation on the spot. But Secretary of State William Seward, with an eye on the possible diplomatic repercussions, begged Lincoln to withhold the proclamation until after McClellan's army had managed to win some significant victory—otherwise, it would be read as a last dying reach by a failing government for anything that looked like a weapon, and the European governments would, under those circumstances, be strongly tempted to intervene to prevent a complete breakdown of law and order. So Lincoln desisted, filing the proclamation away among his papers for the moment.

Inwardly, though, he continued to struggle with the momentous nature of the step he was taking. Abroad, it was assumed to the point of evidence that slave emancipations, unless carefully and gradually managed, would degenerate immediately into race wars, on the order of the 1857 Indian mutiny; at home, the hostile reaction of the border-state representatives to gradual emancipation did not bode well for how immediate emancipation might be received by Northern whites. And Lincoln certainly had no way of predicting which way McClellan and the army were likely to jump, although it was certain that unless he

moved *now* on emancipation, some form of political intervention
by McClellan might make emancipation impossible thereafter.
And so, as the summer of 1862 dragged to a resultless end,
Lincoln's mind turned in a direction unlike that of any other
liberal democrat of the age, and that was to religion.

Lincoln had never demonstrated much interest in religion since
sloughing off his parents' ironclad Calvinism in his youth. He
had never joined a church in Springfield, and one Springfield
clergyman complained that Lincoln was just as likely at "the
railroad shop" at church time and spend "the sabbath in reading
Newspapers, and telling stories to the workmen." It was not that
he took religious questions lightly. In middle age, he softened the
brashness of his youthful "infidelity," and preferred to speak of
himself as struggling "in a twilight, feeling and reasoning my way
through life, as questioning, doubting Thomas did." But if he
had any overarching belief at all, it was his confidence "in the
progress of man and of nations," in "the ultimate triumph of
right, and the overthrow of wrong."

But progress was exactly what this war had defied. Instead of
slavery dying a gradual death, it was bidding for renewal;
instead of the Confederate aristocrats flying the white flag, they
had won victories and were now soliciting international
mediation. Sometime in the fall of 1862, Lincoln tried to line
up these contradictions like a problem in geometry. First, he
postulated, "the will of God prevails"—God could scarcely be
God at all in any other circumstance. Second, "God can not be
for, and against the same thing at the same time." He could not, in
other words, be simultaneously willing both a Northern and a
Southern victory. Hence, he must be willing something else,
"something different from the purpose of either party." The
evidence that God had a higher object in prospect than merely a
military triumph of either side arose from the simple fact that
God, "by his mere quiet power, on the minds of the now
contestants . . . could have either saved or destroyed the Union

without a human contest," or "having begun He could give the final victory to either side any day. Yet the contest proceeds."

He did not finish this proof, but he did not leave much doubt what he thought God now had in mind. "God had decided this question in favor of the slaves," and all the remained was for God to give some sign that it was the time to issue the proclamation. On September 4, Robert E. Lee and the Confederate army splashed across the Potomac into Maryland, aiming for the Northern heartland in central Pennsylvania. "When Lee came over the river," Lincoln said, "I made a solemn vow before God, that if General Lee was driven back ... I would crown the result by the declaration of freedom to the slaves."

Two weeks later, McClellan cautiously challenged Lee at the battle of Antietam, and eked out a marginal victory that forced Lee to retreat back across the Potomac. McClellan showed no desire to pursue Lee to a decisive close. But a marginal victory was victory enough. On September 22, Lincoln brought out his proclamation, read it again to his cabinet, and released it as a presidential order, to become effective on January 1, 1863. Once the proclamation became law, Lincoln remarked to T. J. Barnett, an Indiana judge and a wartime fixture of the Interior Department, "the character of the war will be changed." It might even become a war of "subjugation and extermination." Nevertheless, it was the greatest act of emancipation in that remarkable century of liberal emancipations, towering over the Reform Bill of 1832 and the repeal of the Corn Laws, over the emancipation of Jews in Prussia, Catholics in Britain, and serfs in Russia. It is "my greatest and most enduring contribution to the history of the war," he said, and "as affairs have turned, it is the central act of my administration, and the great event of the nineteenth century."

But there was this peculiar note: he had come to his great act, not as a confident progressive, but as a humble suppliant of the

Divine will, as though liberal democracy required something more than its own secular dynamic to push it past the restraints of race or the exigencies of politics and civil war. It was the first inkling that Lincoln, and liberalism, might need to take different bearings than those gotten solely from the compass of progress.

Chapter 7
Reunion

God and Mr. Lincoln

Lincoln might have thought that the Emancipation Proclamation was a "great event," but there were few people who thought so in the weeks after it was issued. It may well have been a divinely-inspired act of justice, but the Confederates' weapons did not drop from their hands in recognition of that. Even if it helped disrupt the Confederate war effort by enticing Southern slaves to rise up in rebellion, or to flee to the Union lines and freedom, white Northerners were far from pleased at the prospect of hundreds of thousands of refugee slaves appearing on Northern doorsteps or competing for Northern jobs. They were certainly much less easy at the long-threatened spectacle of rebellious black slaves, thirsty for the Proclamation's promised freedom, spitting white Southerners on pitchforks and cane-knives. Nor would Britain, whose massive textile industries were critically dependent on supplies of American cotton, be particularly enthusiastic to witness a rehearsing of the kind of race war it had only just suppressed in India in 1857 and 1858, and that, in turn, could trigger a summons to Lincoln to submit the American war to international arbitration. Well might Richard Cobden stand up in Parliament to hail "the lofty motive of humanity" behind emancipation; the prime minister, Lord Palmerston, believed nevertheless that "the time for making a communication to the United States is evidently coming." Even Lincoln admitted, a week after issuing the preliminary Proclamation in September, that "while commendation in newspapers and by distinguished individuals is all that a vain man could wish, the stocks have declined, and troops come forward more slowly than ever. This, looked soberly in the face, is not very satisfactory." He had offered himself up to the direction of God, and now "I can only trust in God I have made no mistake."

That was small comfort to the more hard-headed members of Lincoln's own party. Congressional elections were scheduled for November 1862, and at both the state and national level, Republicans were cheerlessly felled on all sides. In Lincoln's home state of Illinois, Republicans lost control of both houses of the legislature, and when the new Democrat-dominated legislature assembled in January 1863, its members were right on their feet with hysterical resolutions denouncing emancipation and calling for a negotiated peace:

> WHEREAS the Government of the United States has been engaged
> for nearly two years in an unsuccessful attempt to suppress the
> Southern rebellion . . . and whereas our country is becoming
> almost a nation of widows and orphans, who, if the President's
> emancipation proclamation be carried into effect, will become
> prey to the lusts of freed negroes who will overrun our
> country . . . we are in favor of an immediate suspension of hostilities,
> and recommend the holding of a national convention, for an
> amicable settlement of our difficulties.

In Congress, Lincoln's Republicans held onto their majority. But the most ardent advocates of the emancipation policy were swept away, and the Republican moderates who survived them were going to be instinctively cautious about inviting the wrath of the electorate again.

Neither God nor emancipation seemed to be doing much for the Union armies, either. Once the Emancipation Proclamation was issued, it was clear to Lincoln that the unresponsive and unsympathetic General George McClellan would have to go as the army's commander, and so he did in November 1862. But his replacement, Ambrose Burnside, only led the army to a gigantic and bloody defeat at Fredericksburg, Virginia, in December; and his successor, Joseph Hooker, led them to another defeat, just as embarrassing, at Chancellorsville in May 1863. Each defeat plunged Lincoln deeper into gloom. After the Fredericksburg disaster, Pennsylvania governor Andrew Gregg Curtin remembered that Lincoln "moaned and groaned in anguish. He walked the floor, wringing his hands and uttering exclamations of grief . . . saying over and over again: 'What has God put me in this place for?'"

Yet, it was exactly the conviction that God had put him in that place, which strengthened Lincoln to carry on past all the defeats and criticism of emancipation. One evening his old law partner and mentor, John Todd Stuart, remarked to him, "I have suffered a great deal about this war, of course—my friends and relatives are all in the Southern States. . . . I don't think you or any other man can make it go on just as you wish— I believe that Providence is carrying on this thing." And Lincoln replied "with great emphasis . . . Stuart that is just my opinion." And if Providence was indeed carrying the war forward, Lincoln's task was not to worry about whether it would turn out right, but to carefully observe and calculate all the little ways in which God was arranging the events of the war and interpret them to the people and the politicians. "He believed from the first, I think, that the agitation of Slavery would produce its overthrow," recalled Leonard Swett, and he noticed that Lincoln carried with him "a kind of account book of how things were progressing for three, or four months, and whenever I would get nervous and think things were going wrong, he would get out his estimates and show how everything on the great scale

9. Abraham Lincoln, 1863, by Alexander Gardner.

of action—the resolutions of Legislatures, the instructions of delegates, and things of that character, was going exactly—as he expected."

Lincoln's ability to interpret "the great scale of action" to the American public would turn out to be his greatest asset. His own writing and speaking style had been hammered out on the hard anvil of county courthouses, where clarity, precision, and brevity were key to convincing juries, and he took that passion for persuasion into his public documents as president. That talent for brevity and breadth shone especially in the Gettysburg Address of November 19, 1863. After the terrible Union defeat at Chancellorsville in May 1863, Confederate general Robert E. Lee and his Army of Northern Virginia swung up into Pennsylvania in yet another invasion of the North. Lincoln turned to one more general, a dour Philadelphian named George G. Meade. Meade and the Army of the Potomac stopped Lee's rebels in a massive three-day battle on July 1–3, 1863, at Gettysburg, Pennsylvania, and forced Lee to retreat into Virginia. Lincoln was bitterly disappointed when Meade, like McClellan, failed to pursue and annihilate Lee's battered army. But it was still a victory, and when the Commonwealth of Pennsylvania proposed to create a national soldiers' cemetery at Gettysburg that fall, Lincoln agreed to speak at the dedication ceremonies.

Curiously, Lincoln was not the primary speaker at the Gettysburg cemetery dedication. That role fell to the venerable former governor of Massachusetts and president of Harvard, Edward Everett. Lincoln was allotted only a few minutes to follow Everett's two-and-a-half-hour oration on the history of the war with "a few appropriate remarks." What Lincoln had painstakingly prepared for the occasion, however, was more than appropriate, and there was a time not long ago when it was drilled into the memory of every American schoolchild. *Four score and seven years ago our fathers brought forth on this continent, a new nation, conceived in Liberty, and dedicated to the proposition that all men are created equal.* It was significant that Lincoln dated the birth of the Republic from "four score and seven years"—the date of Declaration of Independence—because for him that document furnished the proposition that was being tested in the war, whether the nation had indeed been founded on "the proposition that all men are created equal." *Now we are engaged in a great civil war, testing whether that nation, or any nation so conceived and so dedicated, can long endure. We are met on a great battle-field of that war. We have come to dedicate a portion of that field, as a final resting place for those who here gave their lives that that nation might live. It is altogether fitting and proper that we should do this.*

However, there was a larger dedication emerging out of the sacrifices of the soldiers, a dedication of the living to the same proposition for which the soldiers had died. *It is for us the living, rather, to be dedicated here to the unfinished work which they who fought here have thus far so nobly advanced. It is rather for us to be here dedicated to the great task remaining before us—that from these honored dead we take increased devotion to that cause for which they gave the last full measure of devotion—that we here highly resolve that these dead shall not have died in vain—that this nation, under God, shall have a new birth of freedom—and that government of the people, by the people, for the people, shall not perish from the earth.* In little more than two hundred words, Lincoln had not only established the priorities of the war but situated every one of his listeners in the cause of furthering the vindication of *government of the people, by the people, for the people.* At the end, poor Edward Everett could only remark, "I should be glad, if I came as near the central idea of the occasion, in two hours, as you did in two minutes."

Lincoln was just as adept at two hours as two minutes, though, something he amply demonstrated in the series of public letters he drafted between August 1862 and August 1863. The letter he wrote for a statewide Republican rally in Springfield, Illinois, on September 3, 1863, may be the best example of these public letters, since Lincoln was tackling in that letter what was, for Illinois the thorniest issue of the war—why it should be fought to emancipate black slaves.

Read aloud at the rally and released simultaneously to the Associated Press, the letter came home like nothing so much as a lawyer's searching cross-examination. "You say you will not fight to free negroes," Lincoln observed, but only to restore the Union; this forgets that every slave who is willing to subtract himself or herself from the Confederate war-making effort by running away to the Union lines, or who is willing to don a Union uniform and carry a rifle against the rebels is just so much more aid in saving the Union. "I thought that in your struggle for the Union, to whatever extent the negroes should cease helping the enemy, to that extent it weakened the enemy in his resistance to you." What grounds, then, did they have for opposing emancipation, since it helped the cause they claimed they were supporting? Truculent whites needed to notice that "Peace does not appear so distant as it did," and when it came, it would be no compliment to white racial supremacy to discover that it was blacks, and not whites, who had saved the republic from dissolution. "There will be some black men who can remember that, with silent tongue, and clenched teeth, and steady eye, and well-poised bayonet, they have helped mankind on to this great consummation, while, I fear," Lincoln continued, "there will be some white ones, unable to forget that, with malignant heart, and deceitful speech, they have strove to hinder it." The next day, the *New York Times* applauded Lincoln's letter vigorously: "President Lincoln's letter to the Springfield Convention has all his characteristic solidity of sense and aptness of expression. It hits, as his written efforts always do, the very heart of the subject."

The campaign of 1864 and reelection

Lincoln was not exaggerating when he said, in the Springfield letter, that peace really did seem to be in the cards during the summer of 1863. After the dreary series of defeats, military and political, that had pressed so bleakly on the North in 1862 and the first half of 1863, the victory at Gettysburg burst up as a spring of refreshment. And then, hard on the heels of Gettysburg, came news that far away on the Mississippi River, General Ulysses S. Grant had forced the surrender of the Confederate citadel at Vicksburg. The "Father of Waters" was back in federal hands.

Lincoln had never met Grant, but he had heard much about him, both good and bad. A year and a half before, it was Grant who had commanded the forces that seized the two key Confederate forts in Tennessee, Fort Henry and Fort Donelson. But then, in April, Grant was caught napping by a rebel army at Shiloh, and Grant's army survived the two-day battle that followed only by the skin of its teeth. People remembered that Grant had been forced to resign from the old Regular Army in the 1850s for alcoholism, and stories began to spread that Grant had been drunk at Shiloh, and was repeatedly drunk on other occasions. Caught in a limbo between fame and disgrace, Grant was given what amounted to occupation duties in northern Mississippi for several months, until he finally gained approval for an operation that would move overland against Vicksburg—and thereby redeem himself.

Lincoln watched Grant's activities with a mixture of apprehension and interest. He appreciated Grant's fighting qualities and his superb organizational abilities. But Lincoln was shy of alcoholics (he himself did not drink at all), and unsure whether he could trust Grant sufficiently to lift him to higher commands. The proposed operation on Vicksburg was a case in point. Lincoln believed that Vicksburg was probably too strong to be taken, and that the best plan was for Grant to bypass the city, secure the remainder of the Mississippi down to New Orleans, and be content with that. But in May, Grant succeeded in landing troops just below the city, pinning its defenders into a siege, and finally compelling their wholesale surrender on the Fourth of July.

Was Grant the general Lincoln needed to win the war? Should he bring him east and give him the command McClellan had fumbled away? Lincoln might have been inclined to do so as early as the summer of 1863. But mistrust over Grant lingered in the air. Besides, when Grant was sounded out informally by a War Department representative about his interest in coming east to take command, even Grant balked. But then, in September, a federal army under William S. Rosecrans walked into a Confederate trap at Chickamauga, in northern Georgia, and was handed one of the worst Union defeats of the war. The remainder of Rosecrans's army was penned back up into the Tennessee river town of Chattanooga by the rebels, and for a while that fall, it looked as though the rebels might be able to pull a Vicksburg in reverse. But again, it was Grant who saved the day. Grant forced open a supply line to Chattanooga along the Tennessee River, and then in November drove the besieging Confederates away from Chattanooga in a great battle along Missionary Ridge.

Vicksburg and Chattanooga together in one year now made the call for Grant to come east irresistible. In December, Congress revived the army rank of lieutenant general (which had been held previously only by George Washington) and in the spring of 1864, Grant came to Washington to receive his commission—and to have the heavy hand of the president laid on him to take up command in the East and finish the work McClellan should have completed two years before. It went without saying that this action came not a moment too soon for Lincoln. Dissatisfaction with the Emancipation Proclamation still bubbled in the public mind; the War Department was imposing a military draft the first time in American history to keep the supply of soldiers coming into uniform, and public opposition to the draft was even angrier than to emancipation; and a presidential election was looming in the fall. Lincoln must have victory, and victory now, or else he had to worry that the people's patience might finally run out on him at the polls.

It is remarkable in this respect that Lincoln never seems once to have considered declaring a national emergency and suspending the national elections of 1864. All through the war, the Northern Democratic opposition screamed without pause over civil liberties violations by Lincoln's administration and the Union military—military arrests of civilians without access to counsel, harassing or shutting down opposition newspapers, suspending the writ of habeas corpus so that suspects could be held indefinitely without trial. And they pilloried Lincoln as a would-be dictator, plotting to make himself king or tyrant or despot, treading on the Constitution and sacrificing American liberty to his own vanity or, in uglier racist terms, to worship of the negro. But looked at in comparison with the record of our own times during war—the Red Scare after World War I, the internment of Japanese Americans during World War II, the McCarthyite scares of the 1950s, and the campus violence of the Vietnam years—Lincoln's record on civil liberties looks almost dangerously indulgent. The total number of verifiable civilian arrests by the administration or the military during the war amounts to no more than 14,000, and the overwhelming percentage of those were in the uncertain border states, where Confederate sympathizers and activists were thick on the ground.

If anything, Lincoln showed himself to be almost overly cautious in his treatment of constitutional issues. The Emancipation Proclamation, remember, had been carefully framed as a military order under the president's war powers. He was meticulous in seeking out legal opinions from his attorney general, Edward Bates, to support actions as commander in chief as minor as the appointment of a temperance representative as an officer or the remission of a fine imposed on a restaurant owner for selling brandy to a wounded soldier. The adoption of policies on the sole ground that "I think the measure politically expedient, and morally right" bothered Lincoln. "Would I not thus give up all footing upon constitution or law? Would I not thus be in the boundless field of absolutism? Would it not lose us ... the very cause we seek to advance?" And he remained so troubled by the constitutionality of the Emancipation Proclamation that in 1864 he began pressuring Congress to write a Thirteenth Amendment to the Constitution, banning slavery for good and for all, rather than merely relying on a war powers proclamation.

Still, if there was ever a time when Lincoln would be tempted to rethink this cautious constitutionalism, it would be the summer of 1864. At the beginning of May, Grant and the Army of the Potomac jumped off toward Richmond, while at the same time, Grant's chief lieutenant, William Tecumseh Sherman, marched another federal army out of Chattanooga, headed for the great Southern rail depot of Atlanta. Three months later, neither of them were close to taking either city. Grant smashed into Lee's rebels in the battle of the Wilderness at the beginning of May and was stunned by the ferocity of Lee's resistance. Unlike his predecessors, Grant refused to back off: he sent word to Lincoln instead that he intended "to fight it out on this line if it takes all summer." But by the end of June, it began to seem as though fighting things out on that line was *all* that was going to happen, and Grant settled into a siege around Richmond that looked like it might have no end. In Georgia, the canny Confederate general, Joseph Johnston, played cat-and-mouse with William Sherman, tick-tacking across the geography of northern Georgia like a chessboard and keeping Atlanta just out of Sherman's reach. The casualty lists mounted, and the objectives were not taken, public opinion sagged dangerously—and the election was getting closer.

Lincoln had no trouble getting the renomination of his own party convention—he was, by that time, too well in control of the party apparatus. But all the signs were pointing to a rejuvenated Democratic party nominating George McClellan for president on a platform that called for an immediate armistice and no more talk about emancipation and the abolition of slavery. "I believe," wrote McClellan, "that a vast majority of our people, whether in the Army & Navy or at home, would with me hail with unbounded joy the permanent restoration of peace on the basis of the Federal Union of the States without the effusion of another drop of blood." By the end of August 1864, the climate looked very bad indeed for Lincoln. John Hay, Lincoln's secretary, found the Democrats "exultant and our own people either growling & despondent or sneakingly apologetic." Years later, Pennsylvania politician Alexander McClure was certain that "there was no period from January 1864, until the 3rd of September of the same year when McClellan would not have defeated Lincoln."

But then the wind abruptly shifted. Confederate president Jefferson Davis removed Joe Johnston from command of the rebel army opposing Sherman and replaced him with the reckless John Bell Hood, who threw his army directly at Sherman. Sherman cheerfully defeated him and forced Hood to abandon Atlanta. At sea, Union admiral David Farragut and a Union squadron shot their way past the forts defending Mobile, Alabama, for a spectacular victory. Northern spirits buoyed up again. On November 8, Election Day, Lincoln won a crushing 55 percent of the popular vote, while Republicans regained secure majorities in both houses of Congress. Long Abe Lincoln, joked *Harper's Weekly*, had just grown a little longer.

And the Confederacy had just grown a little shorter. By the fall of 1864, large portions of the Confederacy's territory were under Union occupation. And while there were still two dangerous Confederate armies on the loose in Virginia and Georgia, the means for supporting, arming, and feeding those armies were shrinking. Over the winter of 1864/65, the hungry rebel armies began to hemorrhage deserters. Demands for individual Southern states to open up peace talks with the North were heard, and in February, Jefferson Davis dispatched three emissaries to meet secretly with Lincoln, hoping to negotiate a peace. Finally, came the unthinkable—Robert E. Lee endorsed the recruiting and arming of black slaves to fight for the Confederacy on the promise of freedom for their service. The question in the minds of everyone as the frosts of winter yielded to the early spring of 1865 was not *whether*, but *when*, the Confederacy would buckle, and what kind of peace should then take place.

Those questions were foremost in Lincoln's mind, too, as he stepped to the podium on the east portico of the Capitol on March 4 to take his second oath of office as president and deliver his Second Inaugural address. The Second Inaugural was far shorter than his first, and this time there were no appeals for the preservation of liberal democracy in the face of a aristocratic "Slave Power." Instead, Lincoln laid out what was almost a theological interpretation of the war, and the principles coming out of that which should guide the peace. What has caused the war, he asked? The answer, coming now after four years, was clear beyond all the political smokescreens of 1861: slavery. "All knew that this interest was, somehow, the cause of the war. To strengthen, perpetuate, and extend this interest was the object for which the insurgents would rend the Union, even by war; while the government claimed no right to do more than to restrict the territorial enlargement of it."

Yet, in Lincoln's view, slavery was only the immediate cause of the war. Behind it, Lincoln discerned a larger, more ultimate cause, the cause of divine justice. For the truth was that slavery was a crime that all Americans had been guilty of, in various ways, all through their history, and the war was the punishment all must receive. God "gives to both North and South, this terrible war . . . until all the wealth piled by the bond-man's two hundred and fifty years of unrequited toil shall be sunk, and until every drop of blood drawn with the lash, shall be paid by another drawn with the sword." Northerners, like the radical Republicans of his own party, might object that the South, not the North, bore the guilt of slavery. But the course of the war had shown something different to Lincoln, that slavery was akin to a national version of original sin, and that God himself had passed sentence upon all. From this God, as from the God of Cromwell's Ironsides, there could be no appeal: "As was said three thousand years ago, so still it must be said 'the judgments of the Lord, are true and righteous altogether.'"

Acknowledging this divine context was Lincoln's fullest confession that the rationality that had given birth to both the Enlightenment and to liberalism had not been enough, just on their own terms, to save democracy in its hour of need. Nor was rationality capable of supplying the elusive qualities of mercy and forgiveness, which he believed were essential to a just reconstruction:

> With malice toward none; with charity for all; with firmness in the right, as God gives us to see the right, let us strive on to finish the work we are in; to bind up the nation's wounds; to care for him who shall have borne the battle, and for his widow, and his orphan—to do all which may achieve and cherish a just, and a lasting peace, among ourselves, and with all nations.

This man of such minimal religious trappings had become the nation's preacher. What he was preaching was not at all what the radical Republicans had in mind for the defeated South. But with an electoral mandate behind him, Lincoln was in charge, and they would have to play by his rules.

Victory and assassination

Three weeks later, the spring thaws set in below Richmond. Grant began probing the Confederate defenses and found them weakened and papery from desertions. Before Grant could stun him with a final blow, Lee gathered what was left of his troops, abandoned Richmond, and fled west. But Grant caught the famished Confederates at Appomattox Court House, and on April 9, 1865, Lee surrendered all that was left of his pitiful army—fewer than 30,000 men. To the South, Sherman had torn his way from Atlanta, through Georgia to Savannah, and then bounded northward into the Carolinas, where he cornered the other Confederate army and was about to force its surrender. The war was finally coming to an end, just in time for Easter, the season of renewal and reconciliation. Lee's surrender came on Palm Sunday, and the following Friday, April 14, was Good Friday. Almost as if to snuff out any supposition that he had lapsed too deeply into his ancestral Calvinism, Lincoln chose to go not to church but to Ford's Theatre, to relax with a comedy of manners titled *Our American Cousin* and to acknowledge the adulation of the packed house.

10. The presidential box at Ford's Theater, where Lincoln was shot by John Wilkes Booth on April 14, 1865.

Shortly after ten o'clock, a prominent Maryland-born actor and sometime Confederate agent named John Wilkes Booth slipped into the presidential box. Desperate to strike what he thought would be the blow that would counterbalance Lee's surrender, Booth aimed a derringer behind Lincoln's head, and shot him behind the left ear. Although doctors were rushed to his side within minutes, Lincoln was probably already brain-dead within ten minutes of the shooting. They kept him breathing, however, and carried him across the street to a boarding house where he could be stretched out on a bed. But this was could be little more than a gesture of devotion. The next morning, at 7:22 a.m., Lincoln's breathing slowed and stopped, and the sixteenth president was dead.

Epilogue

How do we estimate the achievement of Abraham Lincoln? Five days after Lincoln's body was laid to rest in a temporary tomb in his home town of Springfield, Illinois, John Locke Scripps, who had badgered Lincoln into writing his first campaign autobiography, wrote to William Henry Herndon, Lincoln's law partner, with that very question. "In certain showy, and what is said to be, most desirable endowments, how many Americans have surpassed him! Yet how he looms above them now!" marveled Scripps. Lincoln had become "the great American Man—the grand central figure in American (perhaps the World's) History."

But if Lincoln was the Great American Man, there were some very particular ways in which he fulfilled that description. In the largest sense, Lincoln became that Great Man because he saved the American Union. He kept the American republic from following the Bolivarian path of democracy in Latin America and disintegrating into a congeries of petty republican states. In practical terms, this act of cohesion kept the States together as a significant political and economic unit, and ensured that through the following hundred years, it would be able to deploy the concentrated power of that unity to intervene in worldwide crises and to develop a standard of prosperity unmatched by any other great nation.

In ideological terms—and these were the terms most important to Lincoln himself—his leadership ensured that liberal democracy would not be embarrassed by an implosion on the part of its single largest incarnation. "I see a people raising up a Government upon a standard very far in advance of anything that was ever known in the world," Richard Cobden exulted after Lincoln's reelection in 1864, "a people who say, 'We rule ourselves by pure reason; there shall be no religious establishment to guide us or control us; there shall be no born rank of any kind, but every honour held, every promotion enjoyed, shall spring from the people, and by selection; we maintain that we can govern ourselves without the institution of any hierarchy or privileged body whatever.'" All that might have been lost, in America and everywhere else, had the Confederate secession proved that, in fact, human beings could not cooperate by reason, could not govern themselves responsibly, and could not live without one race or class being born, booted and spurred, and ready to ride some other race or class.

Similarly, by his stubborn linkage of liberal politics to free labor, Lincoln made economic mobility and political equality the joint standard by which democratic government was to be measured in the future. Liberalism's great power lay in its abolition of inherited status; but the abolition of status might only produce an equality of nonentities, ruled by some bureaucratic directory, unless equality was confined to the political realm, and the economic sphere opened to the energies of self-transformation. Lincoln had risen from rural poverty to professional success and then to political triumph in a single lifetime, and he was very aware of what that example meant. "There is no permanent class of hired laborers amongst us," Lincoln said in 1859. "Twenty-five years ago, I was a hired laborer. The hired laborer of yesterday, labors on his own account today; and will hire others to labor for him tomorrow."

It only dimly occurred to Lincoln to think that the "hired laborer of yesterday" might manage to put yesterday behind him only because he had accumulated capital, and might discover (as Karl Marx would relentlessly insist) that his capital could be condemned as a theft of surplus value from other hired laborers. But this was an idea Lincoln dismissed out of hand. "That men who are industrious, and sober, and honest in the pursuit of their own interests should after a while accumulate capital ... and hire other people to labor form them is right," Lincoln declared in 1859, the same year that Marx published the first versions of what became *Das Kapital*. The formation of capital through diligence, saving, and work was the true engine of economic mobility, and mobility was what distinguished the free from the slave. "We do not propose any war upon capital," Lincoln announced in 1860, because the accumulation of capital is what permits self-transformation and secures political equality: "we do wish to allow the humblest man an equal chance to get rich with everybody else."

What Lincoln thought—as did Cobden, Bright, Guizot, Tocqueville, and the other liberal lights of the nineteenth century— would pose the greatest danger to democracy was not an insurrection of discontented laborers but the sly maneuverings of a pig-eyed aristocracy to strike up a dark alliance with the working classes, whispering that economic mobility was a chimera and that what the workers needed was subsidy and protection from mobility. "The aristocracy want to frighten the middle classes from the pursuit of reforms," argued John Bright, "and to do this they and their emissaries stimulate a portion of the least wise of the people to menaces and violence, to damage the cause of reform...." Whether this came in the form of a "Slave Power," sneering at the Northern wage laborers as "wage slaves" and whipping up racial fear to bind poor Southern whites to its cause, or in the form of "the mock philanthropy of the

Tory landowners," it was still the same old spirit of crowns and monarchies.

Unhappily, in Tocqueville's France, liberalism was snuffed out by the pseudo-empire of Napoleon III. In England, despite the success of the Reform Bill in 1832 and the repeal of the Corn Laws in 1847, neither Cobden nor Bright ever got their hands on the real levers of power, and the "Tory democracy" of Disraeli largely left the privileges of the aristocracy in place until the First World War. And in Germany, Bismarck's welfare state married the interests of the German social democracy to the rule of the Prussian Junker class so firmly that when middle-class democracy finally arrived in the form of the Weimar Republic, it was born weak and palsied in both spirit and mind, and prey to the rage of a Romantic tyranny.

Lincoln's third achievement may be his most long-lasting, and that is the peculiar way in which he bonded political and moral considerations in a liberal democracy. As the child of the Enlightenment, liberalism was the creature and instrument of reason, and lived by constitutions, statutes, and declarations. But a nation founded (as he put it at Gettysburg) on a *proposition*, and lacking the restraint of unspoken traditions or ancestral custom, can sometimes do the wrong thing with that proposition. It can, in the case of the slaveholding South, insist that the *equality* in that proposition is only an equality of white people; or it can say, in the case of Stephen Douglas, that everyone is entitled to pursue equality in his own way, free from anyone else's objection. Lincoln saw (as perhaps only a man born into a lively religious tradition, which he then distances himself from, emotionally and intellectually, could see) that as much as politics and religion and morality can make a poor marriage, they make for an even worse divorce. For this consistently secular man who never joined a church, there was still no way to speak in America of equality and politics in ways that did not conform to the eternal principles of right and wrong; nor did he hesitate to chart out a path for a political future he did not live to realize by reminding them that the future of liberal democracy had to conform itself, whether it liked it or not, to the dictates of the justice of God.

For Lincoln had, by a long and battlesmoke-stained path, discovered that liberal democracy was not an end in itself, as though merely counting noses was the last word in any political question; nor was it a merely a means that permitted the greatest number to acquire the greatest levels of insipid material contentment. There is evil to be confronted in this world, irrational and spiritualistic as it may sound, and without a willingness to name evil as evil, liberal rationality will stand, hesitating, before the seeming-reasonableness that evil manufactures like a squid's cloud of ink. "Moral principle," Lincoln reminded his fellow opponents of slavery in 1856, "is all that unites us," because if mere economic calculation guided democratic choice, then the economic blandishments of slavery would win every time. To kill slavery, a democracy had to believe it was *wrong*—not just inconvenient or unpopular, but *wrong*. No lesser energy would suffice. No lesser energy, in fact, would ultimately ensure "that this nation under God, shall have a new birth of freedom," since a new birth was, in evangelical terms, the complete renovation and restoration of a peoples' dedication to "government of the people, by the people, for the people," and the only real guarantee that it "shall not perish from the earth."

In an era disenchanted with reason, yet incapable of believing in any form of transcendence except the exalted violence of terrorism, Lincoln's liberalism has the aroma of some old medicine, blended and pounded by hand in an alabaster mortar, unused by those accustomed to quicker and more antiseptic remedies, or dismissed by the angry and the anxious who lack all scale of time. But like those antique potions, it may be the only nostrum under heaven that saves us alive.

References

Introduction

Brogan, Hugh. *Alexis de Tocqueville: A Life*. New Haven: Yale University Press, 2006.

Brooks, Noah. "Personal Recollections of Abraham Lincoln." In *Lincoln Observed: Civil War Dispatches of Noah Brooks*, ed. Michael Burlingame. Baltimore: Johns Hopkins University Press, 1998.

Pratt, Harry E. *The Personal Finances of Abraham Lincoln*. Springfield, IL: Abraham Lincoln Association, 1943.

Russell, William Howard. *My Diary North and South*. New York: Harper, 1863.

Stevens, Walter B. *A Reporter's Lincoln*. Edited by Michael Burlingame. Lincoln: University of Nebraska Press, 1998.

Chapter 1: Equality

"Lamon's Life of Lincoln." *North American Review* 116 (Jan. 1873).

Hammon, Neal O., and Richard Taylor. *Virginia's Western War, 1775–1786*. Mechanicsburg, PA: Stackpole, 2002.

Hobbes, Thomas. *Leviathan*. Edited by W. G. P. Smith. Oxford: Oxford University Press, 1909, 1967.

Jacobson, Douglas L., ed. "Cato's Letters, no. 63" (Feb. 3, 1721). In *The English Libertarian Heritage: From the Writings of John Trenchard and Thomas Gordon in "The Independent Whig" and "Cato's Letters."* Indianapolis, IN: Bobbs-Merrill, 1965.

Paine, Thomas. "Common Sense," *Tracts of the American Revolution, 1763–1776.* Edited by Merrill Jensen. Indianapolis, IN: Hackett, 1967.

Richter, Melvin, ed., *Selected Political Writings* [Montesquieu]. Indianapolis, IN: Hackett, 1990.

Chapter 2: Advancement

Angle, Paul M. *"Here I Have Lived": A History of Lincoln's Springfield.* Chicago: Abraham Lincoln Book Shop, 1971.

Blake, Robert. *Disraeli.* New York: St. Martin's, 1967.

Clark, Christopher. *The Roots of Rural Capitalism: Western Massachusetts, 1780–1860.* Ithaca, NY: Cornell University Press, 1990.

Everett, Edward. "Fourth of July Address at Lowell." In *The American Whigs: An Anthology*, ed. Daniel W. Howe. New York: Wiley, 1973.

Feller, Daniel. *The Jacksonian Promise: America, 1815–1840.* Baltimore: Johns Hopkins University Press, 1995.

Gowing, Richard. *Richard Cobden.* London: Cassell, 1887.

Goodman, Paul. "Ethics and Enterprise: The Values of a Boston Elite, 1800–1860." *American Quarterly* 18 (Autumn 1966).

Jackson, Andrew. "A Political Testament." In *Social Theories of Jacksonian Democracy*, ed. Joseph L. Blau. Indianapolis, IN: Hackett, 2003.

Johnson, Paul. *The Birth of the Modern: World Society, 1815–1830.* New York: Harper Perennial, 1991.

Remini, Robert V. *Henry Clay: Statesman for the Union.* New York: Norton, 1991.

Simon, Paul. *Lincoln's Preparation for Greatness: The Illinois Legislative Years.* Norman: University of Oklahoma Press, 1965.

Speed, Joshua. *Reminiscences of Abraham Lincoln and Notes of a Visit to California.* Louisville, KY: J. P. Morton, 1896.

Taylor of Caroline, John. *Tyranny Unmasked.* Edited by F. Thornton Miller. Indianapolis, IN: Liberty Fund, 1992.

Wilentz, Sean. *Rise of American Democracy: Jefferson to Lincoln.* New York: Norton, 2006.

Chapter 3: Law

Banning, Lance. *The Sacred Fire of Liberty: James Madison and the Founding of the Federal Republic.* Ithaca, NY: Cornell University Press, 1995.

Bauer, K. Jack. *The Mexican War, 1846–1848.* New York: Macmillan, 1974.

Dirck, Brian. *Lincoln the Lawyer.* Urbana: University of Illinois Press, 2007.

Findlay, Paul. *A. Lincoln: The Crucible of Congress.* New York: Crown, 1979.

Hitchcock, Ethan. *Fifty Years in Camp and Field.* Edited by W. A. Croffut. New York: Putnam, 1909.

Holt, Michael F. *The Rise and Fall of the American Whig Party: Jacksonian Politics and the Onset of the Civil War.* New York: Oxford University Press, 1999.

Horwitz, Morton J. *The Transformation of American Law, 1780–1860.* Cambridge, MA: Harvard University Press, 1977.

Howe, Daniel Walker. *What Hath God Wrought: The Transformation of America, 1815–1848.* New York: Oxford University Press, 2007.

"Lincoln Legal Database, Part One." *Lincoln Legal Briefs* 44 (October–December 1997).

Schwartz, Thomas F. "The Springfield Lyceums and Lincoln's 1838 Speech." *Illinois Historical Journal* 83 (Spring 1990).

Seigenthaler, John. *James K. Polk.* New York: Times Books, 2004.

Simon, Paul. *Lincoln's Preparation for Greatness: The Illinois Legislative Years.* Norman: University of Oklahoma Press, 1965.

Steiner, Mark A. *An Honest Calling: The Law Practice of Abraham Lincoln.* DeKalb: Northern Illinois University Press, 2006.

Story, W. W. *Life and Letters of Joseph Story.* Vol. 1. Boston: Little, Brown, 1851.

Thomas, Benjamin P. *Abraham Lincoln: A Biography.* New York: Knopf, 1952.

Wayland, Francis. *The Elements of Political Economy.* Boston: Gould & Lincoln, 1851.

Weik, Jesse W. *The Real Lincoln: A Portrait.* Edited by Michael Burlingame. Lincoln: University of Nebraska Press, 2002.

Winkle, Kenneth. *The Young Eagle: The Rise of Abraham Lincoln.* Dallas, TX: Taylor Trade, 2001.

Wood, Gordon S. *The Radicalism of the American Revolution.*
New York: Knopf, 1992.

Chapter 4: Liberty

Ausubel, Herman. *John Bright: Victorian Reformer.* New York: Wiley,
1966.
Douglas, Stephen A. "The President's Message" (Dec. 9, 1857),
Congressional Globe, 35th Cong., 1st sess.
Fitzhugh, George. *Cannibals All! Or, Slaves Without Masters.*
Edited by C. Vann Woodward. 1856; Cambridge, MA: Belknap
Press of Harvard University Press, 1960.

Chapter 5: Debate

"The Apportionment." *Chicago Press & Tribune*, Nov. 6, 1858.
Carton, Evan. *Patriotic Treason: John Brown and the Soul of America.*
New York: Free Press, 2006.
Douglas, Stephen A. "The Political Campaign in Illinois—
Speech of Mr. Douglas at Chicago." *Washington Union*, July
15, 1858.
———. "The Contest in Illinois—Senator Douglas on Popular
Sovereignty—Extracts from His Speech, Delivered on the Occasion
of His Reception at Chicago, July 9, 1858." *United States
Democratic Review* 42 (August 1858).
Freehling, William W. *The Road to Disunion: Secessionists
Triumphant.* New York: Oxford University Press, 2007.
"From Illinois." *National Era*, Nov. 18, 1858.
Graber, Mark A. *Dred Scott and the Problem of Constitutional
Evil*, 18–20, 182–83. New York: Cambridge University Press,
2006.
Holzer, Harold. *Lincoln at Cooper Union: The Speech that
Made Abraham Lincoln President.* New York: Simon &
Schuster, 2004.
Nevins, Allan, *Ordeal of the Union: A House Dividing, 1852–1857.*
New York: Scribner, 1947.
———. *The Emergence of Lincoln: Prologue to Civil War, 1859–1861.*
New York: Scribner, 1950.
Tarbell, Ida. *Life of Abraham Lincoln.* Vol. 1. New York: Doubleday
& McClure, 1900.

Chapter 6: Emancipation

Browning, Orville Hickman. Diary entry for Dec. 1, 1861. In *Diary of Orville Hickman Browning*, ed. Theodore Calvin Pease and James G. Randall. Vol. 1. Springfield: Trustees of the Illinois State Historical Library, 1925–1933.

Chase, Salmon. Diary entry for Sept. 22. In *Inside Lincoln's Cabinet: The Civil War Diaries of Salmon P. Chase*, ed. David Donald. New York: Longmans, Green, 1954.

Colfax, Schuyler. "Schuyler Colfax to John G. Nicolay, Aug. 26, 1875." In Nicolay-Hay Manuscripts, Illinois State Historical Library.

Donald, David. *Charles Sumner and the Coming of the Civil War*. New York: Knopf, 1960.

Escott, Paul D. *After Secession: Jefferson Davis and the Failure of Confederate Nationalism*. Baton Rouge: Louisiana State University Press, 1978.

Greeley, Horace. Horace Greeley to Abraham Lincoln, July 29, 1861. Abraham Lincoln Papers, Library of Congress.

Luraghi, Raimondo. *A History of the Confederate Navy,*. Translated by Paolo E. Coletta. Annapolis, MD: Naval Institute Press, 1996.

McClellan, George B. George B. McClellan to Lincoln (July 7, 1862). In *The Civil War Papers of George B. McClellan, 1860–1865*, ed. Stephen W. Sears. New York: Ticknor & Fields, 1989.

John Torrey Morse, ed., *Diary of Gideon Welles: Secretary of the Navy under Lincoln and Johnson*. Vol. 1.. New York: Houghton Mifflin, 1911.

"Recognition," *Richmond Daily Dispatch* (July 25, 1861).

Reed, H. Clay. "Lincoln's Compensated Emancipation Plan and Its Relation to Delaware," *Delaware Notes* 7 (1931).

Stephens, Alexander. In *Southern Pamphlets on Secession, November 1860-April 1861*, ed. Jon Wakelyn. Chapel Hill: University of North Carolina Press, 1996.

"The Hon. C. Sumner on a War for Emancipation." *The Anti-Slavery Reporter* (Nov. 1, 1861).

Welles, Gideon. Diary entry for Sept. 22, 1862. In *The Diary of Gideon Welles: Secretary of the Navy under Lincoln and Johnson*, ed. John Torrey Morse. Vol. 1. New York: Houghton Mifflin, 1911.

"What Should Georgia Do?" *Augusta Daily Constitutionalist* (Nov. 16, 1860). In *Southern Editorials on Secession*, ed. Dwight Lowell Dumond. New York: The Century Co., 1931.

Chapter 7: Reunion

Burlingame, Michael. *The Inner World of Abraham Lincoln*. Urbana: University of Illinois Press, 1994.

Cobden, Richard. *Speeches on Questions of Public Policy by Richard Cobden, M.P.* Edited by John Bright and J. E. T. Rogers. London: Macmillan, 1880.

Hay, John. John Hay to John G. Nicolay (Aug. 25, 1864). In *At Lincoln's Side: John Hay's Civil War Correspondence and Selected Writings*, ed. Michael Burlingame. Carbondale: Southern Illinois University Press, 2000.

Jones, Howard. *Abraham Lincoln and a New Birth of Freedom: The Union and Slavery in the Diplomacy of the Civil War*. Lincoln: University of Nebraska Press, 1999.

McClure, Alexander K. *Abraham Lincoln and Men of War-Times*. Philadelphia: The Times Publishing Co., 1892.

Neely, Mark E. *The Fate of Liberty: Abraham Lincoln and Civil Liberties*. New York: Oxford University Press, 1991.

Stuart, John Todd. In *An Oral History of Abraham Lincoln: John G. Nicolay's Interviews and Essays*, ed. Michael Burlingame. Carbondale: Southern Illinois University Press, 1996.

Warren, Louis A. *Lincoln's Gettysburg Declaration: A New Birth of Freedom*. Ft. Wayne, IN: Lincoln National Life Foundation, 1964.

Chapter 8: Epilogue

Ausubel, Herman. *John Bright: Victorian Reformer*. New York: Wiley, 1966.

Morley, John. *The Life of Richard Cobden*. London: Chapman & Hall, 1882.

Beran, Michael Knox. *Forge of Empires, 1861–1871: Three Revolutionary Statesmen and the World They Made*. New York: Free Press, 2007.

Further reading

Introduction

The ultimate reference work on Abraham Lincoln is the *Collected Works of Abraham Lincoln*, edited by Roy F. Basler et al. (New Brunswick, NJ: Rutgers University Press, 1953) in eight volumes, with two supplements. Standing alongside the *Collected Works* is the enormous body of reminiscence material, most of it on Lincoln's early life, taken down by William Henry Herndon in 1865–67, and expanded by Jesse W. Weik, from which Rodney Davis and Douglas Wilson have selected and edited a superb anthology, *Herndon's Informants: Letters, Interviews, and Statements About Abraham Lincoln*, (Urbana: University of Illinois Press, 1998). An older, but still valuable selection from the Herndon-Weik papers was edited by Emmanuel Hertz as *The Hidden Lincoln, From the Letters and Papers of William H. Herndon* (New York: Viking, 1938). Similar to *Herndon's Informants* is the collection of recollected sayings of Lincoln assembled by Don E. and Virginia Fehrenbacher in *Recollected Words of Abraham Lincoln* (Stanford, CA: Stanford University Press, 1996). Also of value are the reminiscence materials collected in David C. Mearns, *The Lincoln Papers* (New York: Doubleday, 1948), and *Conversations with Lincoln*, edited by Charles M. Segal (New Brunswick, NJ: Transaction Publishers, 2002).

For the comparative context of European liberalism, you should look for Pierre Manent, *An Intellectual History of Liberalism* (Princeton, NJ: Princeton University Press, 1994); James J. Sheehan, *German Liberalism in the Nineteenth Century* (Chicago: University of Chicago

Press, 1978); John Morley, *The Life of Richard Cobden* (London: Chapman & Hall, 1882); Herman Ausubel, *John Bright: Victorian Reformer* (New York: Wiley, 1966); and Hugh Brogan, *Alexis de Tocqueville: A Life* (New Haven, CT: Yale University Press, 2006).

Chapter 1: Equality

Any exploration of the Lincoln family genealogy must include Ida M. Tarbell's *In the Footsteps of the Lincolns* (New York: Harper & Bros., 1924). On Thomas Lincoln and his son, and Abraham Lincoln's growth to manhood, *Herndon's Informants* is the indispensable work. But readers will also profit from Michael Burlingame's edition of Walter B. Stevens, *A Reporter's Lincoln* (Lincoln: University of Nebraska Press, 1998) and of interviews conducted by John Nicolay in *An Oral History of Abraham Lincoln: John G. Nicolay's Interviews and Essays* (Carbondale: Southern Illinois University Press, 1996), and from Douglas Wilson's *Honor's Voice: The Transformation of Abraham Lincoln* (New York: Knopf, 1998). The most important works that survey the context in which Lincoln established his basic political loyalties are: Charles G. Sellers, *The Market Revolution: Jacksonian America, 1815–1846* (New York: Oxford University Press, 1991); Sean Wilentz, *Rise of American Democracy: Jefferson to Lincoln* (New York: Norton, 2005); Daniel Walker Howe, *What Hath God Wrought: The Transformation of America, 1815–1848* (New York: Oxford University Press, 2007); and John Ashworth, *Slavery, Capitalism, and Politics in the Antebellum Republic: Volume 1, Commerce and Compromise, 1820–1850* (Cambridge: Cambridge University Press, 1996).

Chapter 2: Advancement

Biographers of Lincoln who wrote in the five decades following Lincoln's death still had access to direct testimony about Lincoln. In this category, the preeminent work is the biography jointly produced by Herndon and Weik, and known simply at *Herndon's Lincoln*, which is now available in a closely edited edition by Rodney Davis and Douglas Wilson (Urbana: University of Illinois Press, 2006). Following after Herndon-Weik, readers will want to consult Josiah G. Holland's *Life of Abraham Lincoln* (Lincoln:

University of Nebraska Press, 1998), Isaac N. Arnold's *The History of Abraham Lincoln and the Overthrow of Slavery* (Chicago: Clarke & Co., 1866), and Arnold's later *The Life of Abraham Lincoln*, in a modern edition by James Rawley (Lincoln: University of Nebraska Press, 1994); Ida Tarbell's *The Life of Abraham Lincoln* (New York: Doubleday & McClure, 1900); and Albert J. Beveridge, *Abraham Lincoln, 1809–1858* (Boston: Houghton Mifflin, 1928).

Appreciating Lincoln's commitment to self-transformation and to the Whig party requires an acquaintance with the chapter on Lincoln in Daniel Walker Howe's *Political Culture of the American Whigs* (Chicago: University of Chicago Press, 1979); Gabor S. Boritt's *Lincoln and the Economics of the American Dream* (Memphis, TN: Memphis State University Press, 1978); Michael F. Holt, *The Rise and Fall of the American Whig Party: Jacksonian Politics and the Onset of the Civil War* (New York: Oxford University Press, 1999); and Robert V. Remini, *Henry Clay: Statesman for the Union* (New York: Norton, 1991). Understanding that transformation against the social and demographic background of Lincoln's Illinois best seen in Kenneth J. Winkle's *The Young Eagle: The Rise of Abraham Lincoln* (Dallas, TX: Taylor Trade Pub., 2001). Lincoln's career in the Illinois legislature is skillfully covered in Paul Simon, *Lincoln's Preparation for Greatness: The Illinois Legislative Years* (Norman: University of Oklahoma Press, 1965) and Paul M. Angle, *"Here I Have Lived": A History of Lincoln's Springfield* (Chicago: Abraham Lincoln Book Shop, 1971).

Chapter 3: Law

Until the creation of the Lincoln Legal Papers Project, most of Lincoln's legal practice was buried in the cabinets and storage trunks of the Illinois courthouses he visited on the Eighth Judicial Circuit. The LLP, however, did a sweeping detective job in unearthing the full breadth of Lincoln's law practice, so sweeping that the complete collection of the documents concerning that practice was committed, not to print but to a two-DVD set: *The Law Practice of Abraham Lincoln: Complete Documentary Edition*, edited by Cullom Davis, Martha Benner, Daniel Stowell et al. (Champaign: University of Illinois Press, 2000). A four volume letter-press edition, containing the documents associated with Lincoln's fifty most important cases was published by the University of Virginia Press in 2008. The LLP, in turn, has made possible two important descriptive studies of Lincoln as a lawyer: Mark A. Steiner, *An Honest Calling: The Law Practice of Abraham Lincoln* (DeKalb: Northern Illinois University Press, 2006) and Brian Dirck, *Lincoln the Lawyer* (Urbana: University of Illinois Press, 2007). A particularly useful narrative by a fellow lawyer is Whitney's *Life on the Circuit with Lincoln*, edited by Paul Angle (Union, NJ: Lawbook Exchange, 2001). The best recent account of Lincoln's term in Congress is Paul Findlay, *A. Lincoln: The Crucible of Congress* (New York: Crown, 1979), while the finest narrative of the Mexican War remains K. Jack Bauer, *The Mexican War, 1846–1848* (New York: Macmillan, 1974).

Chapter 4: Liberty

The definitive book on Lincoln and slavery remains to be written, although a fine start has been made by Lewis E. Lehrman in *Lincoln at Peoria: The Turning Point* (Mechanicsburg, PA: Stackpole Books, 2008). The best overview of Lincoln's thinking on the subject before 1858 is in Benjamin P. Thomas's *Abraham Lincoln: A Biography* (Carbondale: Southern Illinois University Press, 2008) and Michael Burlingame's *The Inner World of Abraham Lincoln* (Urbana: University of Illinois Press, 1994). For Lincoln in the 1850s, the best overviews are in the essays by Don E. Fehrenbacher, collected as *Prelude to Greatness: Lincoln in the 1850s* (Stanford, CA: Stanford University Press, 1962).

Chapter 5: Debate

The Lincoln-Douglas Debates catapulted Lincoln from simple regional prominence to national attention, and opened the path that led him to his great East Coast political debut at the Cooper Union in New York City in February 1860, and his nomination for the presidency months later. The premier account of the Lincoln-Douglas debates is Harry V. Jaffa's *Crisis of the House Divided: An Interpretation of the Issues in the Lincoln-Douglas Debates* (Garden City, NY: Doubleday, 1959). Several free-standing editions of the debates have been published, starting with Lincoln's own edition in 1860, but the two most important are E. Earle Sparks's *The Lincoln-Douglas Debates of 1858* (Springfield: Trustees of the Illinois State Historical Library, 1908) and Rodney Davis and Douglas Wilson's, *The Lincoln-Douglas Debates*

(Urbana: University of Illinois Press, 2008). Lincoln's speech at Cooper Union is ably described in Harold Holzer, *Lincoln at Cooper Union: The Speech that Made Abraham Lincoln President* (New York: Simon & Schuster, 2004) and John M. Corry, *Lincoln at Cooper Union: The Speech That Made Him President* (Philadelphia: Xlibris, 2003).

Chapter 6: Emancipation

The Emancipation Proclamation was regarded by Lincoln as his greatest achievement. Oddly, there has been very little written about the Proclamation, and much of that has been hypercritical of Lincoln for not moving faster, doing more, or manifesting a more modern sensibility on racial issues. (A particularly nasty example of this post facto indictment of Lincoln arrived in 2000 in the form of Lerone Bennett's *Forced Into Glory: Abraham Lincoln's White Dream* (Chicago: Johnson Pub. Co.). The most important reference collection of documents about what is, after all, a political and legal issue is Edward McPherson's *Political History of the United States During the Great Rebellion* (Washington: Philip & Solomons, 1864), while the most detailed narrative is the one written by a participant in the debates over the end of slavery, Henry Wilson, before those debates had even come to their fruition, in Wilson's *History of the Antislavery Measures of the Thirty-Seventh and Thirty-Eighth United-States Congresses, 1861–1864* (Boston: Walker, Wise, 1864).

Lincoln's cabinet contained three diligent diary keepers in Edward Bates, Gideon Welles, and Salmon Chase. Welles's *The Diary of Gideon Welles: Secretary of the Navy under Lincoln and Johnson*, edited by John Torrey Morse (New York: Houghton Mifflin, 1911), is particularly important. But Lincoln's White House staffers also kept up a persistent stream of letters, diary entries, and jottings of various sorts that are also indispensable to understanding the inner workings of his presidency. For these, we are all in the debt of Michael Burlingame for his editions of *At Lincoln's Side: John Hay's Civil War Correspondence and Selected Writings* (Carbondale: Southern Illinois University Press, 2000); William O. Stoddard's *Inside the White House in War Times: Memoirs and Reports of Lincoln's Secretary* (Lincoln: University of Nebraska Press, 2000); *Inside Lincoln's White House: The Complete Civil War Diary of John Hay* (Carbondale: Southern Illinois University Press, 1997); *Lincoln's Journalist: John Hay's Anonymous Writings for the*

Press, 1860–1864 (Carbondale: Southern Illinois University Press, 1998); and *With Lincoln in the White House: Letters, Memoranda, and Other Writings of John G. Nicolay, 1860–1865* (Carbondale: Southern Illinois University Press, 2000). The most important congressional diary—one of the few which survive from the war years, in fact—is the *Diary of Orville Hickman Browning*, edited by Theodore Calvin Pease and James G. Randall (Springfield: Trustees of the Illinois State Historical Library, 1925–1933). The best overall survey of the Lincoln presidency is that by Philip S. Paludan, *The Presidency of Abraham Lincoln* (Lawrence: University of Kansas Press, 1995), although no one should overlook David Herbert Donald's *Lincoln* (New York: Simon & Schuster, 1995) for his coverage of Lincoln's presidential years.

Chapter 7: Reunion

The Gettysburg Address is unquestionably the most written-about of Lincoln's speeches, or perhaps of any American political speech, but the best overall account remains Louis A. Warren's *Lincoln's Gettysburg Declaration: A New Birth of Freedom* (Ft. Wayne, IN: Lincoln National Life Foundation, 1964). Lincoln's plans for Reconstruction have been studied from a number of angles, but the best starting place is Heather Cox Richardson's examination of the overall shape of Republican party domestic policy during the Civil War, *The Greatest Nation of the Earth: Republican Economic Policies During the Civil War* (Cambridge, MA: Harvard University Press, 1997). After that, Herman Belz's *Reconstructing the Union: Theory and Policy during the Civil War* (Ithaca, NY: Cornell University Press, 1969) and William C. Harris's *With Charity for All: Lincoln and the Restoration of the Union* (Lexington: University Press of Kentucky, 1997) assume the place of importance.

The literature on the Lincoln assassination is nearly as large as all the rest of the Lincoln bibliography together. For these purposes, it will suffice to point the reader to a collection of eyewitness accounts, in *We Saw Lincoln Shot: One Hundred Eyewitness Accounts*, edited by Timothy S. Good (Jackson: University Press of Mississippi, 1995), and to George S. Bryan's *The Great American Myth* (reprint, Chicago: Americana House, 1990) and Edward Steers's *Blood on the Moon: The Assassination of Abraham Lincoln* (Lexington: University Press of Kentucky, 2005).

Epilogue

Summing up the significance of Lincoln's life and presidency is a favorite task for those Americans, especially American politicians, who want to "get right with Lincoln." The best estimations, however, come from Lloyd Lewis, *Myths After Lincoln* (New York: Harcourt, Brace, and Co., 1929); Merrill D. Peterson's *Lincoln in American Memory* (New York: Oxford University Press, 1994); and Barry Schwartz, *Abraham Lincoln and the Forge of National Memory* (Chicago: University of Chicago Press, 2000). The only one with a broad European context, however, is Michael Knox Beran, *Forge of Empires, 1861–1871: Three Revolutionary Statesmen and the World They Made* (New York: Free Press, 2007).

Index

Index

Expand your collection of
VERY SHORT INTRODUCTIONS